# GGPlot2 Essentials for Great Data Visualization in R

Alboukadel KASSAMBARA

**Published by Datanovia** (https://www.datanovia.com/en), Alboukadel Kassambara

**Contact**: Alboukadel Kassambara <alboukadel.kassambara@gmail.com>

For general information contact Alboukadel Kassambara <alboukadel.kassambara@gmail.com>.

# Contents

0.1   What you will learn . . . . . . . . . . . . . . . . . . . . . . . . . . . . . . vii
0.2   Key features of this book . . . . . . . . . . . . . . . . . . . . . . . . . . vii
0.3   Book website . . . . . . . . . . . . . . . . . . . . . . . . . . . . . . . . . viii
0.4   Executing the R codes from the PDF . . . . . . . . . . . . . . . . . . . ix
0.5   Colophon . . . . . . . . . . . . . . . . . . . . . . . . . . . . . . . . . . . ix

**About the author**                                                            **x**

**1   Introduction to R**                                                        **1**
1.1   Install R and RStudio . . . . . . . . . . . . . . . . . . . . . . . . . . . 1
1.2   Install and load required R packages . . . . . . . . . . . . . . . . . . . 1
1.3   Data format . . . . . . . . . . . . . . . . . . . . . . . . . . . . . . . . . 2
1.4   Import your data in R . . . . . . . . . . . . . . . . . . . . . . . . . . . 3
1.5   Demo data sets . . . . . . . . . . . . . . . . . . . . . . . . . . . . . . . 3
1.6   Data manipulation . . . . . . . . . . . . . . . . . . . . . . . . . . . . . 4
1.7   Close your R/RStudio session . . . . . . . . . . . . . . . . . . . . . . . 4

**2   Introduction to GGPlot2**                                                  **5**
2.1   What is ggplot2 . . . . . . . . . . . . . . . . . . . . . . . . . . . . . . 5
2.2   Key functions . . . . . . . . . . . . . . . . . . . . . . . . . . . . . . . . 5
2.3   Example of plots . . . . . . . . . . . . . . . . . . . . . . . . . . . . . . 6
2.4   Legend position . . . . . . . . . . . . . . . . . . . . . . . . . . . . . . . 8
2.5   Titles and axis labels . . . . . . . . . . . . . . . . . . . . . . . . . . . . 8
2.6   Facet: Plot with multiple pnels . . . . . . . . . . . . . . . . . . . . . . 9
2.7   GGPlot theme . . . . . . . . . . . . . . . . . . . . . . . . . . . . . . . . 10
2.8   Further customizations of a ggplot . . . . . . . . . . . . . . . . . . . . 11
2.9   Save ggplots . . . . . . . . . . . . . . . . . . . . . . . . . . . . . . . . . 11
2.10  Conclusion . . . . . . . . . . . . . . . . . . . . . . . . . . . . . . . . . . 12

**3   Scatter Plot**                                                             **13**
3.1   Introduction . . . . . . . . . . . . . . . . . . . . . . . . . . . . . . . . . 13
3.2   Data preparation . . . . . . . . . . . . . . . . . . . . . . . . . . . . . . 13
3.3   Loading required R package . . . . . . . . . . . . . . . . . . . . . . . . 14
3.4   Basic scatter plots . . . . . . . . . . . . . . . . . . . . . . . . . . . . . 14
3.5   Scatter plots with multiple groups . . . . . . . . . . . . . . . . . . . . 15
3.6   Add regression lines . . . . . . . . . . . . . . . . . . . . . . . . . . . . . 16
3.7   Add marginal rugs to a scatter plot . . . . . . . . . . . . . . . . . . . 17
3.8   Jitter points to reduce overplotting . . . . . . . . . . . . . . . . . . . . 18
3.9   Add point text labels . . . . . . . . . . . . . . . . . . . . . . . . . . . . 18
3.10  Bubble chart . . . . . . . . . . . . . . . . . . . . . . . . . . . . . . . . . 20

3.11 Color by a continuous variable . . . . . . . . . . . . . . . . . . . . . . 21

**4 Boxplot** **22**
4.1 Introduction . . . . . . . . . . . . . . . . . . . . . . . . . . . . . . . . 22
4.2 Key R functions . . . . . . . . . . . . . . . . . . . . . . . . . . . . . . 22
4.3 Data preparation . . . . . . . . . . . . . . . . . . . . . . . . . . . . . 22
4.4 Loading required R package . . . . . . . . . . . . . . . . . . . . . . . 23
4.5 Basic boxplots . . . . . . . . . . . . . . . . . . . . . . . . . . . . . . 23
4.6 Change boxplot colors by groups: . . . . . . . . . . . . . . . . . . . . 24
4.7 Create a boxplot with multiple groups . . . . . . . . . . . . . . . . . 25
4.8 Multiple panel boxplots . . . . . . . . . . . . . . . . . . . . . . . . . 25
4.9 Conclusion . . . . . . . . . . . . . . . . . . . . . . . . . . . . . . . . 26

**5 Violin Plot** **27**
5.1 Introduction . . . . . . . . . . . . . . . . . . . . . . . . . . . . . . . . 27
5.2 Key R functions . . . . . . . . . . . . . . . . . . . . . . . . . . . . . . 27
5.3 Data preparation . . . . . . . . . . . . . . . . . . . . . . . . . . . . . 27
5.4 Loading required R package . . . . . . . . . . . . . . . . . . . . . . . 28
5.5 Basic violin plots . . . . . . . . . . . . . . . . . . . . . . . . . . . . . 28
5.6 Create a Violin Plot with multiple groups . . . . . . . . . . . . . . . 29
5.7 Conclusion . . . . . . . . . . . . . . . . . . . . . . . . . . . . . . . . 30

**6 Dot Plot** **31**
6.1 Introduction . . . . . . . . . . . . . . . . . . . . . . . . . . . . . . . . 31
6.2 Key R functions . . . . . . . . . . . . . . . . . . . . . . . . . . . . . . 31
6.3 Data preparation . . . . . . . . . . . . . . . . . . . . . . . . . . . . . 31
6.4 Loading required R package . . . . . . . . . . . . . . . . . . . . . . . 32
6.5 Basic Dot Plots . . . . . . . . . . . . . . . . . . . . . . . . . . . . . . 32
6.6 Create a Dot Plot with multiple groups . . . . . . . . . . . . . . . . 33
6.7 Conclusion . . . . . . . . . . . . . . . . . . . . . . . . . . . . . . . . 34

**7 Stripcharts** **35**
7.1 Introduction . . . . . . . . . . . . . . . . . . . . . . . . . . . . . . . . 35
7.2 Key R functions . . . . . . . . . . . . . . . . . . . . . . . . . . . . . . 35
7.3 Data preparation . . . . . . . . . . . . . . . . . . . . . . . . . . . . . 35
7.4 Loading required R package . . . . . . . . . . . . . . . . . . . . . . . 36
7.5 Basic stripcharts . . . . . . . . . . . . . . . . . . . . . . . . . . . . . 36
7.6 Combine with box plots and violin plots . . . . . . . . . . . . . . . . 37
7.7 Create a stripchart with multiple groups . . . . . . . . . . . . . . . . 37
7.8 Conclusion . . . . . . . . . . . . . . . . . . . . . . . . . . . . . . . . 38

**8 Line Plot** **39**
8.1 Introduction . . . . . . . . . . . . . . . . . . . . . . . . . . . . . . . . 39
8.2 Key R functions . . . . . . . . . . . . . . . . . . . . . . . . . . . . . . 39
8.3 Data preparation . . . . . . . . . . . . . . . . . . . . . . . . . . . . . 39
8.4 Loading required R package . . . . . . . . . . . . . . . . . . . . . . . 40
8.5 Basic line plots . . . . . . . . . . . . . . . . . . . . . . . . . . . . . . 40
8.6 Line plot with multiple groups . . . . . . . . . . . . . . . . . . . . . 41
8.7 Line plot with a numeric x-axis . . . . . . . . . . . . . . . . . . . . . 41
8.8 Line plot with dates on x-axis: Time series . . . . . . . . . . . . . . 42
8.9 Conclusion . . . . . . . . . . . . . . . . . . . . . . . . . . . . . . . . 44

**9  Barplot**                                                                                **45**
  9.1   Key R functions . . . . . . . . . . . . . . . . . . . . . . . . . . . .   45
  9.2   Data preparation . . . . . . . . . . . . . . . . . . . . . . . . . . .   45
  9.3   Loading required R package . . . . . . . . . . . . . . . . . . . . . .   46
  9.4   Basic barplots . . . . . . . . . . . . . . . . . . . . . . . . . . . .   46
  9.5   Change barplot colors by groups . . . . . . . . . . . . . . . . . . .   47
  9.6   Barplot with multiple groups . . . . . . . . . . . . . . . . . . . . .   47
  9.7   Conclusion . . . . . . . . . . . . . . . . . . . . . . . . . . . . . .   50

**10  Error Bars**                                                                            **51**
  10.1   Introduction . . . . . . . . . . . . . . . . . . . . . . . . . . . .   51
  10.2   Loading required R package . . . . . . . . . . . . . . . . . . . . .   51
  10.3   Data preparation . . . . . . . . . . . . . . . . . . . . . . . . . .   51
  10.4   Key R functions and error plot types . . . . . . . . . . . . . . . .   52
  10.5   Basic error bars . . . . . . . . . . . . . . . . . . . . . . . . . .   53
  10.6   Grouped error bars . . . . . . . . . . . . . . . . . . . . . . . . .   56
  10.7   Conclusion . . . . . . . . . . . . . . . . . . . . . . . . . . . . .   59

**11  Density Plot**                                                                          **60**
  11.1   Key R functions . . . . . . . . . . . . . . . . . . . . . . . . . .   60
  11.2   Data preparation . . . . . . . . . . . . . . . . . . . . . . . . . .   60
  11.3   Loading required R package . . . . . . . . . . . . . . . . . . . . .   61
  11.4   Basic density plots . . . . . . . . . . . . . . . . . . . . . . . . .   61
  11.5   Change color by groups . . . . . . . . . . . . . . . . . . . . . . .   62

**12  Histogram Plot**                                                                        **63**
  12.1   Key R functions . . . . . . . . . . . . . . . . . . . . . . . . . .   63
  12.2   Data preparation . . . . . . . . . . . . . . . . . . . . . . . . . .   63
  12.3   Loading required R package . . . . . . . . . . . . . . . . . . . . .   64
  12.4   Basic histogram plots . . . . . . . . . . . . . . . . . . . . . . . .   64
  12.5   Change color by groups . . . . . . . . . . . . . . . . . . . . . . .   65
  12.6   Combine histogram and density plots . . . . . . . . . . . . . . . . .   66
  12.7   Conclusion . . . . . . . . . . . . . . . . . . . . . . . . . . . . .   67

**13  QQPlot**                                                                                **68**
  13.1   Key R functions . . . . . . . . . . . . . . . . . . . . . . . . . .   68
  13.2   Data preparation . . . . . . . . . . . . . . . . . . . . . . . . . .   68
  13.3   Loading required R package . . . . . . . . . . . . . . . . . . . . .   68
  13.4   Create qqplots . . . . . . . . . . . . . . . . . . . . . . . . . . .   69
  13.5   Conclusion . . . . . . . . . . . . . . . . . . . . . . . . . . . . .   70

**14  ECDF Plot**                                                                             **71**
  14.1   Data preparation . . . . . . . . . . . . . . . . . . . . . . . . . .   71
  14.2   Loading required R package . . . . . . . . . . . . . . . . . . . . .   71
  14.3   Create ECDF plots . . . . . . . . . . . . . . . . . . . . . . . . . .   72
  14.4   Conclusion . . . . . . . . . . . . . . . . . . . . . . . . . . . . .   72

**15  Multiple GGPlots into a Figure**                                                        **73**
  15.1   Introduction . . . . . . . . . . . . . . . . . . . . . . . . . . . .   73
  15.2   Loading required R packages . . . . . . . . . . . . . . . . . . . . .   73
  15.3   Basic ggplot . . . . . . . . . . . . . . . . . . . . . . . . . . . .   73

15.4  Multiple panels figure using ggplot facet . . . . . . . . . . . . . . . . . . . . 74
15.5  Combine multiple ggplots using ggarrange() . . . . . . . . . . . . . . . . . . 76
15.6  Conclusion   . . . . . . . . . . . . . . . . . . . . . . . . . . . . . . . . . . 80

# Preface

## 0.1 What you will learn

**GGPlot2** is a powerful and a flexible R package, implemented by Hadley Wickham, for producing elegant graphics piece by piece.

ggplot2 has become a popular package for data visualization. The official documentation of the package is available at: `https://ggplot2.tidyverse.org/reference/`. However, going through this comprehensive documentation can "drive you crazy"!

This book presents the essentials of ggplot2 to easily create beautiful graphics in R.

## 0.2 Key features of this book

- Covers the most important graphic functions
- Short, self-contained chapters with practical examples.

Some examples of graphs, described in this book, are shown below.

- Create **Scatter plots** to display the relationship between two continuous variables x and y

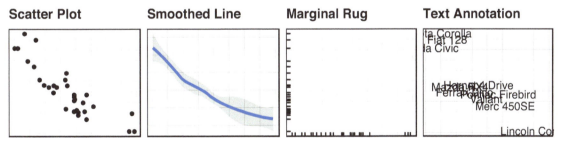

- Using Box plots and alternatives to visualize data grouped by the levels of a categorical variable

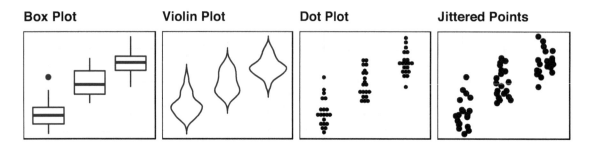

- Bar and Line Plots

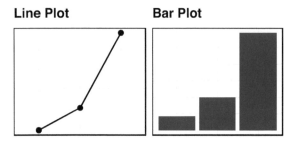

- Visualizing error bars

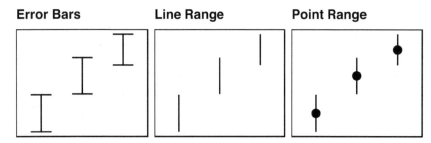

- Inspecting the distribution of a **continuous variable** using **density plots**, **histograms** and alternatives

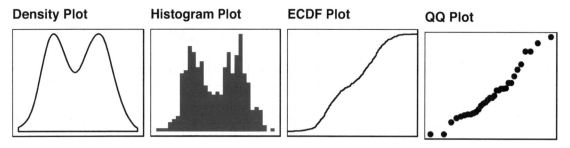

You will also learn how to combine multiple ggplots into one figure.

## 0.3   Book website

The website for this book is located at : `https://www.datanovia.com/en/`. It contains number of resources.

## 0.4 Executing the R codes from the PDF

For a single line R code, you can just copy the code from the PDF to the R console.

For a multiple-line R codes, an error is generated, sometimes, when you copy and paste directly the R code from the PDF to the R console. If this happens, a solution is to:

- Paste firstly the code in your R code editor or in your text editor
- Copy the code from your text/code editor to the R console

## 0.5 Colophon

This book was built with R 3.3.2 and the following packages :

```
##         name version                  source
## 1 bookdown   0.9.1 Github:rstudio/bookdown
## 2  cowplot   0.9.4                    CRAN
## 3    dplyr   0.8.3                    CRAN
## 4    dplyr   0.8.3                    CRAN
## 5 ggplot2    3.2.0                    CRAN
## 6   ggpubr   0.2.4                    CRAN
## 7  ggrepel   0.8.0                    CRAN
## 8    readr   1.3.1                    CRAN
```

# About the author

Alboukadel Kassambara is a PhD in Bioinformatics and Cancer Biology. He works since many years on genomic data analysis and visualization (read more: `http://www.alboukadel.com/`).

He has work experiences in statistical and computational methods to identify prognostic and predictive biomarker signatures through integrative analysis of large-scale genomic and clinical data sets.

He is the author of:

1) the bioinformatics tool named **GenomicScape** (www.genomicscape.com), an easy-to-use web tool for gene expression data analysis and visualization.

2) the **Datanovia** (`https://www.datanovia.com/en/`) and **STHDA** (`http://www.sthda.com/english/`) websites, which contains many courses and **tutorials** on data data mining and statistics for decision supports.

3) many popular **R packages** for multivariate data analysis, survival analysis, correlation matrix visualization and basic data visualization (`https://rpkgs.datanovia.com/`).

4) many **books** on data analysis, visualization and machine learning (`https://www.datanovia.com/en/shop/`)

# Chapter 1

# Introduction to R

**R** is a free and powerful statistical software for **analyzing** and **visualizing** data. If you want to learn easily the essential of R programming, visit our series of tutorials available on STHDA: http://www.sthda.com/english/wiki/r-basics-quick-and-easy.

In this chapter, we provide a very brief introduction to **R**, for installing R/RStudio as well as importing your data into R and installing required libraries.

## 1.1  Install R and RStudio

R and RStudio can be installed on Windows, MAC OSX and Linux platforms. RStudio is an integrated development environment for R that makes using R easier. It includes a console, code editor and tools for plotting.

1. R can be downloaded and installed from the Comprehensive R Archive Network (CRAN) webpage (http://cran.r-project.org/)
2. After installing R software, install also the RStudio software available at: http://www.rstudio.com/products/RStudio/.
3. Launch RStudio and start use R inside R studio.

## 1.2  Install and load required R packages

An R package is a collection of functionalities that extends the capabilities of base R. For example, to use the R code provide in this book, you should install the following R packages:

- `tidyverse` packages, which are a collection of R packages that share the same programming philosophy. These packages include:
    - `readr`: for importing data into R
    - `dplyr`: for data manipulation
    - `ggplot2`: for data visualization.
- `ggpubr` package, which makes it easy, for beginner, to create publication ready plots.

1. **Install the tidyverse package**. Installing tidyverse will install automatically readr, dplyr, ggplot2 and more. Type the following code in the R console:

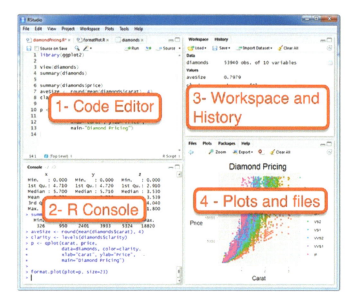

**Figure 1.1:** Rstudio interface

```r
install.packages("tidyverse")
```

2. **Install the ggpubr package**.

```r
install.packages("ggpubr")
```

3. **Load required packages**. After installation, you must first load the package for using the functions in the package. The function **library()** is used for this task. An alternative function is **require()**. For example, to load ggplot2 and ggpubr packages, type this:

```r
library("ggplot2")
library("ggpubr")
```

Now, we can use R functions, such as *ggscatter*() [in the ggpubr package] for creating a scatter plot.

If you want a help about a given function, say ggscatter(), type this in R console: **?ggscatter**.

## 1.3  Data format

Your data should be in rectangular format, where columns are variables and rows are observations (individuals or samples).

- Column names should be compatible with R naming conventions. Avoid column with blank space and special characters. Good column names: **long_jump** or **long.jump**. Bad column name: **long jump**.

- Avoid beginning column names with a number. Use letter instead. Good column names: **sport_100m** or **x100m**. Bad column name: **100m**.

- Replace missing values by **NA** (for not available)

For example, your data should look like this:

```
  manufacturer model displ year cyl      trans drv
1         audi    a4   1.8 1999   4   auto(l5)   f
2         audi    a4   1.8 1999   4 manual(m5)   f
3         audi    a4   2.0 2008   4 manual(m6)   f
4         audi    a4   2.0 2008   4   auto(av)   f
```

Read more at: Best Practices in Preparing Data Files for Importing into R[1]

## 1.4 Import your data in R

First, save your data into txt or csv file formats and import it as follow (you will be asked to choose the file):

```r
library("readr")

# Reads tab delimited files (.txt tab)
my_data <- read_tsv(file.choose())

# Reads comma (,) delimited files (.csv)
my_data <- read_csv(file.choose())

# Reads semicolon(;) separated files(.csv)
my_data <- read_csv2(file.choose())
```

Read more about how to import data into R at this link: http://www.sthda.com/english/wiki/importing-data-into-r

## 1.5 Demo data sets

R comes with several demo data sets for playing with R functions. The most used R demo data sets include: **USArrests**, **iris** and **mtcars**. To load a demo data set, use the function **data()** as follow. The function **head()** is used to inspect the data.

```r
data("iris")   # Loading
head(iris, n = 3)   # Print the first n = 3 rows
```

```
##   Sepal.Length Sepal.Width Petal.Length Petal.Width Species
## 1          5.1         3.5          1.4         0.2  setosa
## 2          4.9         3.0          1.4         0.2  setosa
## 3          4.7         3.2          1.3         0.2  setosa
```

To learn more about iris data sets, type this:

```r
?iris
```

After typing the above R code, you will see the description of **iris** data set: this iris data set gives the measurements in centimeters of the variables sepal length and width and petal length

---

[1] http://www.sthda.com/english/wiki/best-practices-in-preparing-data-files-for-importing-into-r

and width, respectively, for 50 flowers from each of 3 species of iris. The species are Iris setosa, versicolor, and virginica.

## 1.6   Data manipulation

After importing your data in R, you can easily manipulate it using the `dplyr` package (**?**), which can be installed using the R code: `install.packages("dplyr")`.

After loading dplyr, you can use the following R functions:

- `filter()`: Pick rows (observations/samples) based on their values.
- `distinct()`: Remove duplicate rows.
- `arrange()`: Reorder the rows.
- `select()`: Select columns (variables) by their names.
- `rename()`: Rename columns.
- `mutate()`: Add/create new variables.
- `summarise()`: Compute statistical summaries (e.g., computing the mean or the sum)
- `group_by()`: Operate on subsets of the data set.

> Note that, dplyr package allows to use the forward-pipe chaining operator (%>%) for combining multiple operations. For example, x %>% f is equivalent to f(x). Using the pipe (%>%), the output of each operation is passed to the next operation. This makes R programming easy.

Read more about Data Manipulation at this link: `https://www.datanovia.com/en/courses/data-manipulation-in-r/`

## 1.7   Close your R/RStudio session

Each time you close R/RStudio, you will be asked whether you want to save the data from your R session. If you decide to save, the data will be available in future R sessions.

# Chapter 2

# Introduction to GGPlot2

## 2.1 What is ggplot2

**GGPlot2** is a powerful and a flexible R package, implemented by Hadley Wickham, for producing elegant graphics piece by piece (Wickham et al., 2019).

The **gg** in ggplot2 means *Grammar of Graphics*, a graphic concept which describes plots by using a "grammar". According to the ggplot2 concept, a plot can be divided into different fundamental parts: **Plot = data + Aesthetics + Geometry**

- **data**: a data frame
- **aesthetics**: used to indicate the **x** and **y** variables. It can be also used to control the **color**, the **size** and the **shape** of points, etc.....
- **geometry**: corresponds to the type of graphics (histogram, box plot, line plot, ....)

The ggplot2 syntax might seem opaque for beginners, but once you understand the basics, you can create and customize any kind of plots you want.

Note that, to reduce this opacity, we recently created an R package, named **ggpubr** (ggplot2 Based Publication Ready Plots), for making ggplot simpler for students and researchers with non-advanced programming backgrounds.

## 2.2 Key functions

After installing and loading the ggplot2 package, you can use the following key functions:

| Plot types | GGPlot2 functions |
|---|---|
| Initialize a ggplot | ggplot() |
| Scatter plot | geom_point() |
| Box plot | geom_boxplot() |
| Violin plot | geom_violin() |
| strip chart | geom_jitter() |
| Dot plot | geom_dotplot() |
| Bar chart | geom_bar() or geom_col() |
| Line plot | geom_line() |

| Plot types | GGPlot2 functions |
|---|---|
| Histogram | geom_histogram() |
| Density plot | geom_density() |
| Error bars | geom_errorbar() |
| QQ plot | stat_qq() |
| ECDF plot | stat_ecdf() |
| Title and axis labels | labs() |

## 2.3   Example of plots

The main function in the ggplot2 package is `ggplot()`, which can be used to initialize the plotting system with data and x/y variables.

For example, the following R code takes the `iris` data set to initialize the ggplot and then a layer (`geom_point()`) is added onto the ggplot to create a scatter plot of x = `Sepal.Length` by y = `Sepal.Width`:

```
library(ggplot2)
ggplot(iris, aes(x = Sepal.Length, y = Sepal.Width))+
  geom_point()
```

```
# Change point size, color and shape
ggplot(iris, aes(x = Sepal.Length, y = Sepal.Width))+
  geom_point(size = 1.2, color = "steelblue", shape = 21)
```

Note that, in the code above, the shape of points is specified as number. The different point shape available in R, include:

## Point shapes available in R

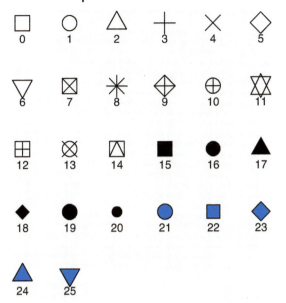

It's also possible to control points shape and color by a grouping variable (here, `Species`). For example, in the code below, we map points color and shape to the `Species` grouping variable.

Note that, a ggplot can be holded in a variable, say `p`, to be printed later

```r
# Control points color by groups
ggplot(iris, aes(x = Sepal.Length, y = Sepal.Width))+
  geom_point(aes(color = Species, shape = Species))

# Change the default color manually.
# Use the scale_color_manual() function
p <- ggplot(iris, aes(x = Sepal.Length, y = Sepal.Width))+
  geom_point(aes(color = Species, shape = Species))+
  scale_color_manual(values = c("#00AFBB", "#E7B800", "#FC4E07"))
print(p)
```

## 2.4   Legend position

The default legend position is "right".  Use the function `theme()` with the argument `legend.position` to specify the legend position.

Allowed values for the legend position include: "left", "top", "right", "bottom", "none".

Examples:

```
# Change legend position to the top
p + theme(legend.position = "top")
```

To remove legend, use `p + theme(legend.position = "none")`.

## 2.5   Titles and axis labels

The function `labs()` can be used to change easily the main title, the subtitle, the axis labels and captions.

```
p + labs(
  title = "Edgar Anderson's Iris Data",
  subtitle = "iris is a data frame with 150 cases (rows) and 5 variables",
  x = "Sepal Length (cm)", y = "Sepal Width (cm)"
  )
```

**Edgar Anderson's Iris Data**

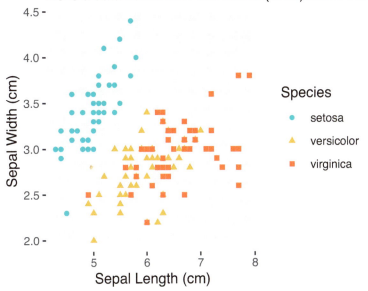

## 2.6 Facet: Plot with multiple pnels

You can also split the plot into multiple panels according to a grouping variable. R function: `facet_wrap()`. Another interesting feature of ggplot2, is the possibility to combine multiple layers on the same plot. For example, with the following R code, we'll:

- Add points with `geom_point()`, colored by groups.
- Add the fitted smoothed regression line using `geom_smooth()`. By default the function `geom_smooth()` add the regression line and the confidence area. You can control the line color and confidence area fill color by groups.
- Facet the plot into multiple panels by groups
- Change color and fill manually using the function `scale_color_manual()` and `scale_fill_manual()`

```
ggplot(iris, aes(x = Sepal.Length, y = Sepal.Width))+
  geom_point(aes(color = Species))+
  geom_smooth(aes(color = Species, fill = Species))+
  facet_wrap(~Species, ncol = 3, nrow = 1)+
  scale_color_manual(values = c("#00AFBB", "#E7B800", "#FC4E07"))+
  scale_fill_manual(values = c("#00AFBB", "#E7B800", "#FC4E07"))
```

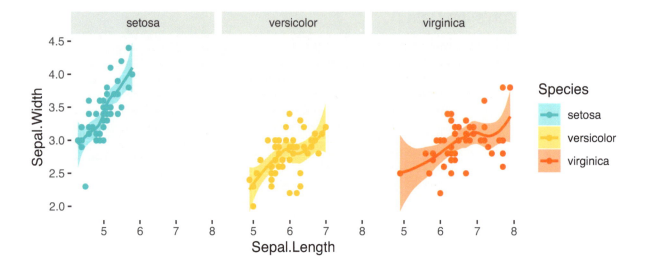

## 2.7   GGPlot theme

Note that, the default theme of ggplots is `theme_gray()` (or `theme_grey()`), which is theme with grey background and white grid lines. More themes are available for professional presentations or publications. These include: `theme_bw()`, `theme_classic()` and `theme_minimal()`.

To change the theme of a given ggplot (p), use this: `p + theme_classic()`. To change the default theme to `theme_classic()` for all the future ggplots during your entire R session, type the following R code:

```r
theme_set(
  theme_classic()
)
```

Now you can create ggplots with `theme_classic()` as default theme:

```r
ggplot(iris, aes(x = Sepal.Length, y = Sepal.Width))+
  geom_point()
```

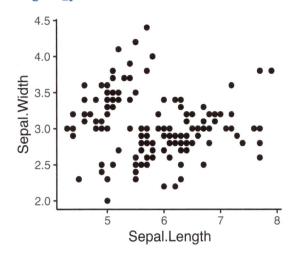

## 2.8 Further customizations of a ggplot

You can read more in our online ggplot cheatsheet, GGPlot Cheat Sheet for Great Customization[1], which describes how to:

- Add title, subtitle, caption and change axis labels
- Change the appearance - color, size and face - of titles
- Set the axis limits
- Set a logarithmic axis scale
- Rotate axis text labels
- Change the legend title and position, as well, as the color and the size
- Change a ggplot theme and modify the background color
- Add a background image to a ggplot
- Use different color palettes: custom color palettes, color-blind friendly palettes, RColorBrewer palettes, viridis color palettes and scientific journal color palettes.
- Change point shapes (plotting symbols) and line types
- Rotate a ggplot
- Annotate a ggplot by adding straight lines, arrows, rectangles and text.

## 2.9 Save ggplots

You can export a ggplot to many file formats, including: PDF, SVG vector files, PNG, TIFF, JPEG, etc.

The standard procedure to save any graphics from R is as follow:

1. **Open a graphic device** using one of the following functions:

- pdf("r-graphics.pdf"),
- svg("r-graphics.svg"),
- png("r-graphics.png"),
- tiff("r-graphics.tiff"),
- jpeg("r-graphics.jpg"),
- and so on.

Additional arguments indicating the width and the height (in inches) of the graphics region can be also specified in the mentioned function.

2. **Create and print a plot**

3. **Close the graphic device** using the function `dev.off()`

For example, to export ggplot2 graphs to a pdf file, the R code looks like this:

```
# Create some plots
library(ggplot2)
myplot1 <- ggplot(iris, aes(Sepal.Length, Sepal.Width)) +
  geom_point()
myplot2 <- ggplot(iris, aes(Species, Sepal.Length)) +
  geom_boxplot()
```

---

[1]http://www.sthda.com/english/articles/32-r-graphics-essentials/125-ggplot-cheat-sheet-for-great-customization/

```r
# Print plots to a pdf file
pdf("ggplot.pdf")
print(myplot1)      # Plot 1 --> in the first page of PDF
print(myplot2)      # Plot 2 ---> in the second page of the PDF
dev.off()
```

For printing to a **png** file, use:

```r
png("myplot.png")
print(myplot)
dev.off()
```

It's also possible to make a ggplot and to save it from the screen using the function **ggsave()**:

```r
# 1. Create a plot: displayed on the screen (by default)
ggplot(mtcars, aes(wt, mpg)) + geom_point()
# 2.1. Save the plot to a pdf
ggsave("myplot.pdf")
# 2.2 OR save it to png file
ggsave("myplot.png")
```

## 2.10   Conclusion

This article explains the basics of ggplot2 and shows how to export a ggplot to a PDF or PNG file.

# Chapter 3

# Scatter Plot

## 3.1  Introduction

A **Scatter plot** (also known as **X-Y plot** or **Point graph**) is used to display the relationship between two continuous variables x and y.

By displaying a variable in each axis, it is possible to determine if an association or a *correlation* exists between the two variables.

The correlation can be: positive (values increase together), negative (one value decreases as the other increases), null (no correlation), linear, exponential and U-shaped.

This article describes how to create scatter plots in R using the ggplot2 package.

You will learn how to:

- Color points by groups
- Create bubble charts
- Add regression line to a scatter plot

## 3.2  Data preparation

Demo dataset: `mtcars`. The variable `cyl` is used as grouping variable.

```
# Load data
data("mtcars")
df <- mtcars

# Convert cyl as a grouping variable
df$cyl <- as.factor(df$cyl)

# Inspect the data
head(df[, c("wt", "mpg", "cyl", "qsec")], 4)

##                  wt  mpg cyl qsec
## Mazda RX4      2.62 21.0   6 16.5
## Mazda RX4 Wag  2.88 21.0   6 17.0
```

```
## Datsun 710      2.32 22.8   4 18.6
## Hornet 4 Drive 3.21 21.4   6 19.4
```

## 3.3   Loading required R package

Load the ggplot2 package and set the default theme to `theme_bw()` with the legend at the top of the plot:

```r
library(ggplot2)
theme_set(
  theme_bw() +
    theme(legend.position = "top")
  )
```

## 3.4   Basic scatter plots

- Key functions: `geom_point()` for creating scatter plots.
- Key arguments: `color`, `size` and `shape` to change point color, size and shape.

```r
# Initiate a ggplot
b <- ggplot(df, aes(x = wt, y = mpg))

# Basic scatter plot
b + geom_point()

# Change color, shape and size
b + geom_point(color = "#00AFBB", size = 2, shape = 23)
```

The different point shapes commonly used in R, include:

## Point shapes available in R

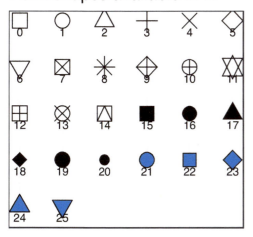

## 3.5 Scatter plots with multiple groups

This section describes how to change point colors and shapes by groups. The functions `scale_color_manual()` and `scale_shape_manual()` are used to manually customize the color and the shape of points, respectively.

In the R code below, point shapes and colors are controlled by the levels of the grouping variable *cyl* :

```
# Change point shapes by the levels of cyl
b + geom_point(aes(shape = cyl))

# Change point shapes and colors by the levels of cyl
# Set custom colors
b + geom_point(aes(shape = cyl, color = cyl)) +
  scale_color_manual(values = c("#00AFBB", "#E7B800", "#FC4E07"))
```

## 3.6    Add regression lines

- Key R function: `geom_smooth()` for adding smoothed conditional means / regression line.
- Key arguments:
    - `color`, `size` and `linetype`: Change the line color, size and type.
    - `fill`: Change the fill color of the confidence region.

A simplified format of the function 'geom_smooth():

```
geom_smooth(method="auto", se=TRUE, fullrange=FALSE, level=0.95)
```

> - **method** : smoothing method to be used.  Possible values are lm, glm, gam, loess, rlm.
>     - **method = "loess"**: This is the default value for small number of observations. It computes a smooth local regression.  You can read more about **loess** using the R code **?loess**.
>     - **method = "lm"**: It fits a **linear model**.  Note that, it's also possible to indicate the formula as **formula = y ~ poly(x, 3)** to specify a degree 3 polynomial.
> - **se** : logical value. If TRUE, confidence interval is displayed around smooth.
> - **fullrange** : logical value. If TRUE, the fit spans the full range of the plot
> - **level** : level of confidence interval to use. Default value is 0.95

To add a regression line on a scatter plot, the function `geom_smooth()` is used in combination with the argument `method = lm`. lm stands for linear model.

```
# Add regression line
b + geom_point() + geom_smooth(method = lm)

# Point + regression line
# Remove the confidence interval
b + geom_point() +
  geom_smooth(method = lm, se = FALSE)

# loess method: local regression fitting
b + geom_point() + geom_smooth()
```

**Change point color and shapes by groups:**

```
# Change color and shape by groups (cyl)
b + geom_point(aes(color = cyl, shape=cyl)) +
```

```r
  geom_smooth(aes(color = cyl, fill = cyl), method = lm) +
  scale_color_manual(values = c("#00AFBB", "#E7B800", "#FC4E07"))+
  scale_fill_manual(values = c("#00AFBB", "#E7B800", "#FC4E07"))

# Remove confidence intervals
# Extend the regression lines: fullrange
b + geom_point(aes(color = cyl, shape = cyl)) +
  geom_smooth(aes(color = cyl), method = lm, se = FALSE, fullrange = TRUE) +
    scale_color_manual(values = c("#00AFBB", "#E7B800", "#FC4E07"))+
  scale_fill_manual(values = c("#00AFBB", "#E7B800", "#FC4E07"))
```

## 3.7   Add marginal rugs to a scatter plot

The function `geom_rug()` is used to display display individual cases on the plot.

```r
# Add marginal rugs
b + geom_point() + geom_rug()

# Change colors by groups
b + geom_point(aes(color = cyl)) +
  geom_rug(aes(color = cyl))

# Add marginal rugs using faithful data
data(faithful)
ggplot(faithful, aes(x = eruptions, y = waiting)) +
  geom_point() + geom_rug()
```

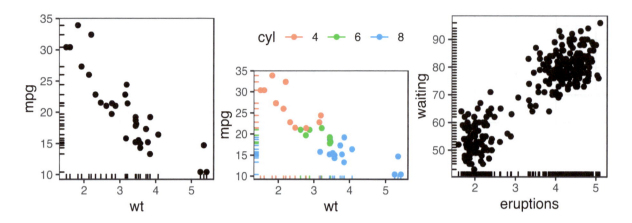

## 3.8  Jitter points to reduce overplotting

The `mpg` data set [in **ggplot2**] is used in the following examples.

To reduce overplotting, the option `position = position_jitter()` with the arguments *width* and *height* are used:

- *width*: degree of jitter in x direction.
- *height*: degree of jitter in y direction.

```
# Default plot
ggplot(mpg, aes(displ, hwy)) +
  geom_point()
```

```
# Use jitter to reduce overplotting
ggplot(mpg, aes(displ, hwy)) +
  geom_point(position = position_jitter(width = 0.5, height = 0.5))
```

## 3.9  Add point text labels

Key functions:

- `geom_text()` and `geom_label()`: ggplot2 standard functions to add text to a plot.

- `geom_text_repel()` and `geom_label_repel()` [in ggrepel package]. Repulsive textual annotations. Avoid text overlapping.

First install ggrepel (`install.packages("ggrepel")`), then type this:

```
library(ggrepel)
```

```
# Add text to the plot
.labs <- rownames(df)
b + geom_point(aes(color = cyl)) +
  geom_text_repel(aes(label = .labs,  color = cyl), size = 3)+
  scale_color_manual(values = c("#00AFBB", "#E7B800", "#FC4E07"))
```

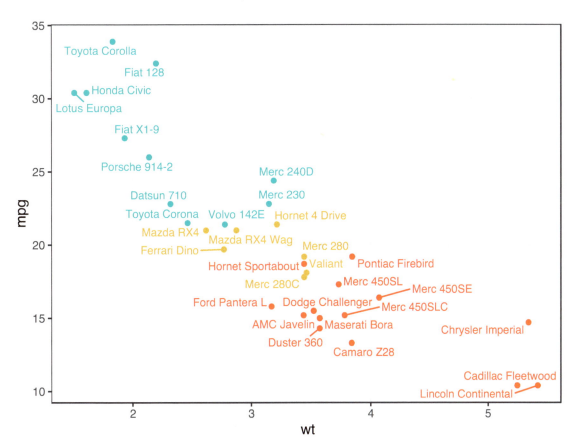

```
# Draw a rectangle underneath the text, making it easier to read.
b + geom_point(aes(color = cyl)) +
  geom_label_repel(aes(label = .labs,  color = cyl), size = 3)+
  scale_color_manual(values = c("#00AFBB", "#E7B800", "#FC4E07"))
```

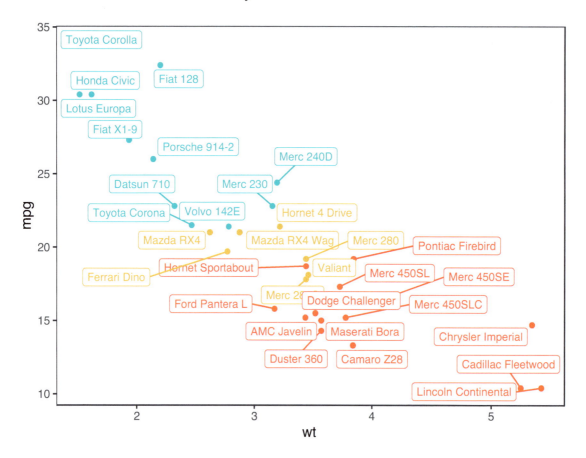

## 3.10   Bubble chart

In a bubble chart, points `size` is controlled by a continuous variable, here `qsec`. In the R code below, the argument alpha is used to control color transparency.  alpha should be between 0 and 1.

```
b + geom_point(aes(color = cyl, size = qsec), alpha = 0.5) +
  scale_color_manual(values = c("#00AFBB", "#E7B800", "#FC4E07")) +
  scale_size(range = c(0.5, 12))   # Adjust the range of points size
```

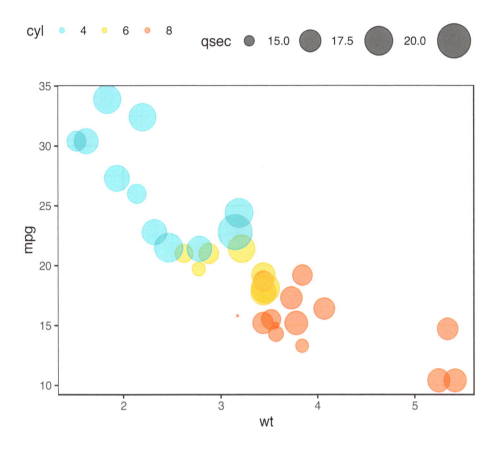

## 3.11 Color by a continuous variable

- Color points according to the values of the continuous variable: "mpg".
- Change the default blue gradient color using the function `scale_color_gradientn()` [in ggplot2], by specifying two or more colors.

```
b + geom_point(aes(color = mpg), size = 3) +
  scale_color_gradientn(colors = c("#00AFBB", "#E7B800", "#FC4E07")) +
  theme(legend.position = "right")
```

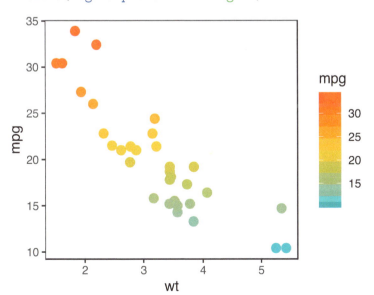

# Chapter 4

# Boxplot

## 4.1 Introduction

**Boxplots** (or **Box plots**) are used to visualize the distribution of a grouped continuous variable through their quartiles.

Box Plots have the advantage of taking up less space compared to Histogram and Density plot. This is useful when comparing distributions between many groups.

Visualizing data using boxplots makes it possible to:

- Inspect the key values of the data, including: the average, median, first and third quartiles, etc
- Identify potential outliers in the data
- See whether the data is tightly grouped, symmetrical or skewed, etc

This article describes how to create and customize **boxplot** using the **ggplot2** R package.

## 4.2 Key R functions

- Key R function: `geom_boxplot()` [ggplot2 package]
- Key arguments to customize the plot:
  - `width`: the width of the box plot
  - `notch`: logical. If TRUE, creates a **notched boxplot**. The notch displays a confidence interval around the median which is normally based on the `median +/- 1.58*IQR/sqrt(n)`. Notches are used to compare groups; if the notches of two boxes do not overlap, this is a strong evidence that the medians differ.
  - `color`, `size`, `linetype`: Border line color, size and type
  - `fill`: box plot areas fill color
  - `outlier.colour`, `outlier.shape`, `outlier.size`: The color, the shape and the size for outlying points.

## 4.3 Data preparation

- Demo dataset: `ToothGrowth`

- Continuous variable: `len` (tooth length). Used on y-axis
- Grouping variable: `dose` (dose levels of vitamin C: 0.5, 1, and 2 mg/day). Used on x-axis.

First, convert the variable `dose` from a numeric to a discrete factor variable:

```r
data("ToothGrowth")
ToothGrowth$dose <- as.factor(ToothGrowth$dose)
head(ToothGrowth, 4)

##     len supp dose
## 1  4.2   VC  0.5
## 2 11.5   VC  0.5
## 3  7.3   VC  0.5
## 4  5.8   VC  0.5
```

## 4.4   Loading required R package

Load the ggplot2 package and set the default theme to `theme_classic()` with the legend at the top of the plot:

```r
library(ggplot2)
theme_set(
  theme_classic() +
    theme(legend.position = "top")
)
```

## 4.5   Basic boxplots

We start by initiating a plot named e, then we'll add layers:

```r
# Default plot
e <- ggplot(ToothGrowth, aes(x = dose, y = len))
e + geom_boxplot()

# Notched box plot with mean points
e + geom_boxplot(notch = TRUE, fill = "lightgray")+
  stat_summary(fun.y = mean, geom = "point",
               shape = 18, size = 2.5, color = "#FC4E07")
```

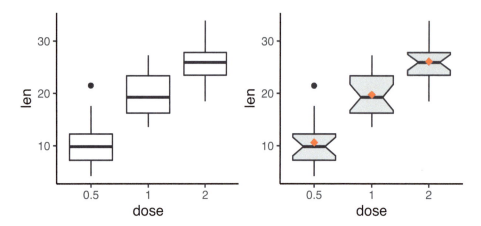

Note that, it's possible to use the function `scale_x_discrete()` for:

- choosing which items to display: for example c("0.5", "2"),
- changing the order of items: for example from c("0.5", "1", "2") to c("2", "0.5", "1")

For example, type this:

```
# Choose which items to display: group "0.5" and "2"
e + geom_boxplot() +
  scale_x_discrete(limits=c("0.5", "2"))
```

```
# Change the default order of items
e + geom_boxplot() +
  scale_x_discrete(limits=c("2", "0.5", "1"))
```

## 4.6   Change boxplot colors by groups:

The following R code will change the boxplot line and fill color. The functions `scale_color_manual()` and `scale_fill_manual()` are used to specify custom colors for each group.

```
# Color by group (dose)
e + geom_boxplot(aes(color = dose))+
  scale_color_manual(values = c("#00AFBB", "#E7B800", "#FC4E07"))
```

```
# Change fill color by group (dose)
e + geom_boxplot(aes(fill = dose)) +
  scale_fill_manual(values = c("#00AFBB", "#E7B800", "#FC4E07"))
```

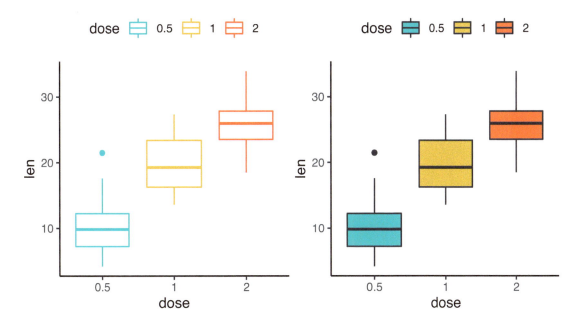

## 4.7  Create a boxplot with multiple groups

Two different grouping variables are used: `dose` on x-axis and `supp` as fill color (legend variable).

The space between the grouped box plots is adjusted using the function `position_dodge()`.

```
e2 <- e +
  geom_boxplot(aes(fill = supp), position = position_dodge(0.9) ) +
  scale_fill_manual(values = c("#999999", "#E69F00"))
e2
```

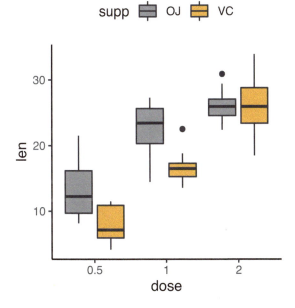

## 4.8  Multiple panel boxplots

You can split the plot into multiple panel using the function `facet_wrap()`:

```
e2 + facet_wrap(~supp)
```

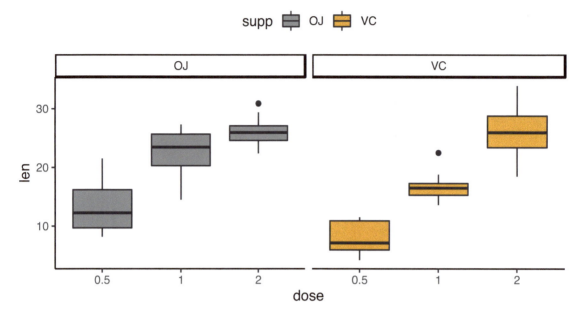

## 4.9   Conclusion

This article describes how to create a boxplot using the ggplot2 package.

# Chapter 5

# Violin Plot

## 5.1 Introduction

A **Violin Plot** is used to visualize the distribution of the data and its probability density.

This chart is a combination of a Box plot and a Density Plot that is rotated and placed on each side, to display the distribution shape of the data.

Typically, violin plots will include a marker for the median of the data and a box indicating the interquartile range, as in standard boxplots.

A Violin Plot shows more information than a Box Plot. For example, in a violin plot, you can see whether the distribution of the data is bimodal or multimodal.

This article describes how to create and customize **violin plots** using the **ggplot2** R package.

## 5.2 Key R functions

Key function:

- `geom_violin()`: Creates violin plots. Key arguments:
  - `color`, `size`, `linetype`: Border line color, size and type
  - `fill`: Areas fill color
  - `trim`: logical value. If TRUE (default), trim the tails of the violins to the range of the data. If FALSE, don't trim the tails.
- `stat_summary()`: Adds summary statistics (mean, median, ...) on the violin plots.

## 5.3 Data preparation

- Demo dataset: `ToothGrowth`
  - Continuous variable: `len` (tooth length). Used on y-axis
  - Grouping variable: `dose` (dose levels of vitamin C: 0.5, 1, and 2 mg/day). Used on x-axis.

First, convert the variable `dose` from a numeric to a discrete factor variable:

```
data("ToothGrowth")
ToothGrowth$dose <- as.factor(ToothGrowth$dose)
head(ToothGrowth, 4)
```

```
##     len supp dose
## 1  4.2   VC  0.5
## 2 11.5   VC  0.5
## 3  7.3   VC  0.5
## 4  5.8   VC  0.5
```

## 5.4   Loading required R package

Load the ggplot2 package and set the default theme to `theme_classic()` with the legend at the top of the plot:

```
library(ggplot2)
theme_set(
  theme_classic() +
    theme(legend.position = "top")
  )
```

## 5.5   Basic violin plots

We start by initiating a plot named **e**, then we'll add layers. The following R code creates Violin Plots combined with summary statistics (mean +/- SD) and Box Plots.

Create basic violin plots with summary statistics:

```
# Initiate a ggplot
e <- ggplot(ToothGrowth, aes(x = dose, y = len))

# Add mean points +/- SD
# Use geom = "pointrange" or geom = "crossbar"
e + geom_violin(trim = FALSE) +
  stat_summary(
    fun.data = "mean_sdl",  fun.args = list(mult = 1),
    geom = "pointrange", color = "black"
    )

# Combine with box plot to add median and quartiles
# Change fill color by groups, remove legend
e + geom_violin(aes(fill = dose), trim = FALSE) +
  geom_boxplot(width = 0.2)+
  scale_fill_manual(values = c("#00AFBB", "#E7B800", "#FC4E07"))+
  theme(legend.position = "none")
```

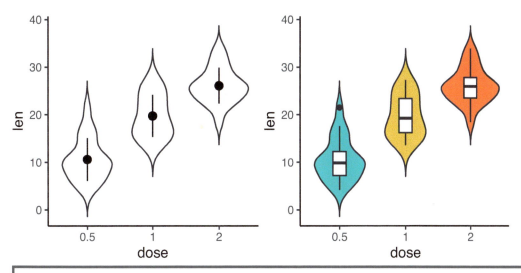

The function `mean_sdl` is used for adding mean and standard deviation. It computes the mean plus or minus a constant times the standard deviation. In the R code above, the constant is specified using the argument `mult` (mult = 1). By default mult = 2. The mean +/- SD can be added as a crossbar or a pointrange.

## 5.6 Create a Violin Plot with multiple groups

Two different grouping variables are used: `dose` on x-axis and `supp` as line color (legend variable).

The space between the grouped plots is adjusted using the function `position_dodge()`.

```
e + geom_violin(aes(color = supp), trim = FALSE, position = position_dodge(0.9) ) +
  geom_boxplot(aes(color = supp), width = 0.15, position = position_dodge(0.9)) +
  scale_color_manual(values = c("#00AFBB", "#E7B800"))
```

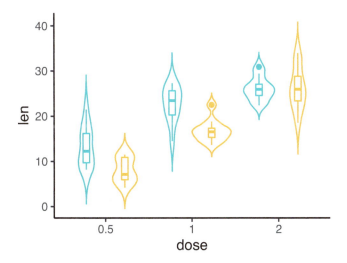

## 5.7   Conclusion

This article describes how to create a Violin Plot using the ggplot2 package.

# Chapter 6

# Dot Plot

## 6.1 Introduction

A **Dot Plot** is used to visualize the distribution of the data. This chart creates stacked dots, where each dot represents one observation.

Summary statistics are usually added to dotplots for indicating, for example, the median of the data and the interquartile range.

This article describes how to create and customize **Dot Plots** using the **ggplot2** R package.

## 6.2 Key R functions

- Key function: `geom_dotplot()`. Creates stacked dots, with each dot representing one observation.
- Key arguments:
  - `stackdir`: which direction to stack the dots. "up" (default), "down", "center", "centerwhole" (centered, but with dots aligned).
  - `stackratio`: how close to stack the dots. Default is 1, where dots just just touch. Use smaller values for closer, overlapping dots.
  - `color`, `fill`: Dot border color and area fill
  - `dotsize`: The diameter of the dots relative to binwidth, default 1.

## 6.3 Data preparation

- Demo dataset: `ToothGrowth`
  - Continuous variable: `len` (tooth length). Used on y-axis
  - Grouping variable: `dose` (dose levels of vitamin C: 0.5, 1, and 2 mg/day). Used on x-axis.

First, convert the variable `dose` from a numeric to a discrete factor variable:

```
data("ToothGrowth")
ToothGrowth$dose <- as.factor(ToothGrowth$dose)
head(ToothGrowth, 4)
```

```
##     len supp dose
## 1  4.2   VC  0.5
## 2 11.5   VC  0.5
## 3  7.3   VC  0.5
## 4  5.8   VC  0.5
```

## 6.4   Loading required R package

Load the ggplot2 package and set the default theme to `theme_classic()` with the legend at the top of the plot:

```
library(ggplot2)
theme_set(
  theme_classic() +
    theme(legend.position = "top")
  )
```

## 6.5   Basic Dot Plots

We start by initiating a plot named e, then we'll add layers. The following R code creates dotplots combined with summary statistics (mean +/- SD), boxplots and violin plots.

```
# Initiate a ggplot
e <- ggplot(ToothGrowth, aes(x = dose, y = len))

# Dotplot with summary statistics: mean +/- SD
e + geom_dotplot(binaxis = "y", stackdir = "center", fill = "lightgray") +
  stat_summary(fun.data = "mean_sdl", fun.args = list(mult=1))

# dot plots combined with box plots
e + geom_boxplot(width = 0.5) +
  geom_dotplot(binaxis = "y", stackdir = "center", fill = "lightgray")

# Dot plot + violin plot + stat summary
e + geom_violin(trim = FALSE) +
  geom_dotplot(binaxis='y', stackdir='center', fill = "#999999") +
  stat_summary(fun.data="mean_sdl",  fun.args = list(mult=1))
```

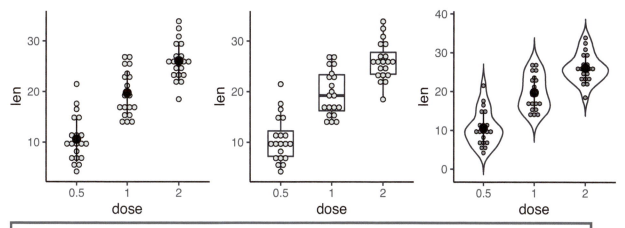

> The function `mean_sdl` is used for adding mean and standard deviation. It computes the mean plus or minus a constant times the standard deviation. In the R code above, the constant is specified using the argument `mult` (mult = 1). By default mult = 2. The mean +/- SD can be added as a crossbar or a pointrange.

## 6.6 Create a Dot Plot with multiple groups

Two different grouping variables are used: `dose` on x-axis and `supp` as color (legend variable).

The space between the grouped plots is adjusted using the function `position_dodge()`.

```
# Change dots fill color by groups
e + geom_boxplot(width = 0.5) +
  geom_dotplot(aes(fill = supp), binaxis='y', stackdir='center')+
  scale_fill_manual(values = c("#00AFBB", "#E7B800"))

# Change the position : interval between dot plot of the same group
e + geom_boxplot(aes(color = supp), width = 0.5, position = position_dodge(0.8)) +
  geom_dotplot(aes(fill = supp, color = supp), binaxis='y', stackdir='center',
               dotsize = 0.8,position = position_dodge(0.8))+
  scale_fill_manual(values = c("#00AFBB", "#E7B800"))+
  scale_color_manual(values = c("#00AFBB", "#E7B800"))
```

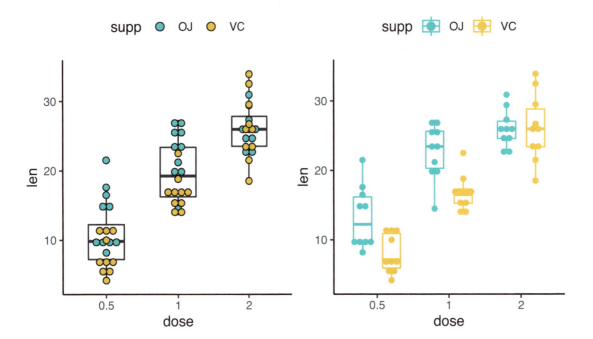

## 6.7   Conclusion

This article describes how to create a Dot Plot using the ggplot2 package.

# Chapter 7

# Stripcharts

## 7.1 Introduction

**Stripcharts** are also known as one dimensional scatter plots. These plots are suitable compared to box plots when sample sizes are small.

This article describes how to create and customize **Stripcharts** using the **ggplot2** R package.

## 7.2 Key R functions

- Key function: `geom_jitter()`
- key arguments: `color`, `fill`, `size`, `shape`. Changes points color, fill, size and shape

## 7.3 Data preparation

- Demo dataset: `ToothGrowth`
  - Continuous variable: `len` (tooth length). Used on y-axis
  - Grouping variable: `dose` (dose levels of vitamin C: 0.5, 1, and 2 mg/day). Used on x-axis.

First, convert the variable `dose` from a numeric to a discrete factor variable:

```r
data("ToothGrowth")
ToothGrowth$dose <- as.factor(ToothGrowth$dose)
head(ToothGrowth, 3)
```

```
##     len supp dose
## 1   4.2   VC  0.5
## 2  11.5   VC  0.5
## 3   7.3   VC  0.5
```

## 7.4   Loading required R package

Load the ggplot2 package and set the default theme to `theme_classic()` with the legend at the top of the plot:

```
library(ggplot2)
theme_set(
  theme_classic() +
    theme(legend.position = "top")
)
```

## 7.5   Basic stripcharts

We start by initiating a plot named **e**, then we'll add layers. The following R code creates stripcharts combined with summary statistics (mean +/- SD), boxplots and violin plots.

- Change points shape and color by groups
- Adjust the degree of jittering: `position_jitter(0.2)`
- Add summary statistics:

```
# Initiate a ggplot
e <- ggplot(ToothGrowth, aes(x = dose, y = len))

# Stripcharts with summary statistics
# Change color by dose groups
e + geom_jitter(aes(shape = dose, color = dose),
                position = position_jitter(0.2), size = 1.2) +
  stat_summary(aes(color = dose), size = 0.4,
               fun.data="mean_sdl",  fun.args = list(mult=1))+
  scale_color_manual(values =  c("#00AFBB", "#E7B800", "#FC4E07"))
```

The function `mean_sdl` is used for adding mean and standard deviation. It computes the mean plus or minus a constant times the standard deviation. In the R code above, the constant is specified using the argument `mult` (mult = 1). By default mult = 2. The mean +/- SD can be added as a crossbar or a pointrange.

## 7.6 Combine with box plots and violin plots

```
# Combine with box plot
e + geom_boxplot() +
  geom_jitter(position = position_jitter(0.2))
```

```
# Strip chart + violin plot + stat summary
e + geom_violin(trim = FALSE) +
  geom_jitter(position = position_jitter(0.2)) +
  stat_summary(fun.data="mean_sdl",  fun.args = list(mult=1),
               color = "red")
```

## 7.7 Create a stripchart with multiple groups

The R code is similar to what we have seen in dot plots section. However, to create dodged jitter points, you should use the function `position_jitterdodge()` instead of `position_dodge()`.

```
e + geom_jitter(
  aes(shape = supp, color = supp), size = 1.2,
  position = position_jitterdodge(jitter.width = 0.2, dodge.width = 0.8)
  ) +
  stat_summary(
    aes(color = supp), fun.data="mean_sdl", fun.args = list(mult=1),
    size = 0.4, position = position_dodge(0.8)
    )+
  scale_color_manual(values =  c("#00AFBB", "#E7B800"))
```

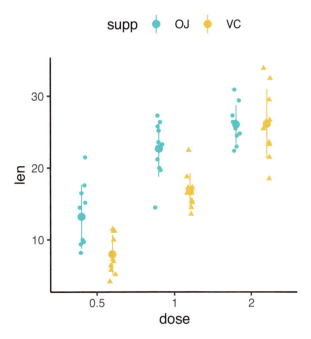

## 7.8   Conclusion

This article describes how to create a stripchart using the ggplot2 package.

# Chapter 8

# Line Plot

## 8.1 Introduction

In a **line plot**, observations are ordered by x value and connected by a line.

x value (for x axis) can be :

- date : for a time series data
- texts
- discrete numeric values
- continuous numeric values

This article describes how to create a line plot using the ggplot2 R package

You will learn how to:

- Create basic and grouped line plots
- Add points to a line plot
- Change the line types and colors by group

## 8.2 Key R functions

- Key functions:
  - `geom_path()` connects the observations in the order in which they appear in the data.
  - `geom_line()` connects them in order of the variable on the x axis.
  - `geom_step()` creates a stairstep plot, highlighting exactly when changes occur.
- Key arguments to customize the plot: alpha, color, linetype and size

## 8.3 Data preparation

We'll create two data frames derived from the `ToothGrowth` datasets.

```
df <- data.frame(dose=c("D0.5", "D1", "D2"),
                 len=c(4.2, 10, 29.5))
```

```r
head(df, 4)
```

```
##   dose  len
## 1 D0.5  4.2
## 2   D1 10.0
## 3   D2 29.5
```

```r
df2 <- data.frame(supp=rep(c("VC", "OJ"), each=3),
                  dose=rep(c("D0.5", "D1", "D2"),2),
                  len=c(6.8, 15, 33, 4.2, 10, 29.5))
```

```r
head(df2, 4)
```

```
##   supp dose  len
## 1   VC D0.5  6.8
## 2   VC   D1 15.0
## 3   VC   D2 33.0
## 4   OJ D0.5  4.2
```

- `len`: Tooth length
- `dose`: Dose in milligrams (0.5, 1, 2)
- `supp`: Supplement type (VC or OJ)

## 8.4   Loading required R package

Load the ggplot2 package and set the default theme to `theme_classic()` with the legend at the top of the plot:

```r
library(ggplot2)
theme_set(
  theme_classic() +
    theme(legend.position = "top")
  )
```

## 8.5   Basic line plots

```r
p <- ggplot(data = df, aes(x = dose, y = len, group = 1))
# Basic line plot with points
 p + geom_line() + geom_point()

# Change line type and color
p + geom_line(linetype = "dashed", color = "steelblue")+
  geom_point(color = "steelblue")

# Use geom_step()
p + geom_step() + geom_point()
```

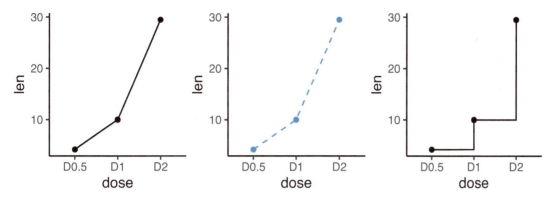

Note that, the group aesthetic determines which cases are connected together.

## 8.6 Line plot with multiple groups

In the graphs below, line types and point shapes are controlled automatically by the levels of the variable `supp`:

```
p <- ggplot(df2, aes(x = dose, y = len, group = supp))
# Change line types and point shapes by groups
p + geom_line(aes(linetype = supp)) +
    geom_point(aes(shape = supp))

# Change line types, point shapes and colors
# Change color manually: custom color
p + geom_line(aes(linetype = supp, color = supp))+
    geom_point(aes(shape = supp, color = supp)) +
    scale_color_manual(values=c("#999999", "#E69F00"))
```

## 8.7 Line plot with a numeric x-axis

If the variable on x-axis is numeric, it can be useful to treat it as a continuous or a factor variable depending on what you want to do:

```
# Create some data
df3 <- data.frame(supp=rep(c("VC", "OJ"), each=3),
```

```
                      dose=rep(c("0.5", "1", "2"),2),
                      len=c(6.8, 15, 33, 4.2, 10, 29.5))
head(df3)
```

```
##    supp dose  len
## 1   VC  0.5  6.8
## 2   VC    1 15.0
## 3   VC    2 33.0
## 4   OJ  0.5  4.2
## 5   OJ    1 10.0
## 6   OJ    2 29.5
```

```
# x axis treated as continuous variable
df3$dose <- as.numeric(as.vector(df3$dose))
ggplot(data = df3, aes(x = dose, y = len, group = supp, color = supp)) +
  geom_line() + geom_point()
```

```
# Axis treated as discrete variable
df3$dose<-as.factor(df3$dose)
ggplot(data=df3, aes(x = dose, y = len, group = supp, color = supp)) +
  geom_line() + geom_point()
```

## 8.8   Line plot with dates on x-axis:  Time series

economics time series data sets are used :

```
head(economics)
```

```
## # A tibble: 6 x 6
##   date         pce     pop psavert uempmed unemploy
##   <date>     <dbl>   <dbl>   <dbl>   <dbl>    <dbl>
## 1 1967-07-01  507. 198712    12.6     4.5     2944
## 2 1967-08-01  510. 198911    12.6     4.7     2945
## 3 1967-09-01  516. 199113    11.9     4.6     2958
## 4 1967-10-01  512. 199311    12.9     4.9     3143
## 5 1967-11-01  517. 199498    12.8     4.7     3066
## 6 1967-12-01  525. 199657    11.8     4.8     3018
```

Plots :

```r
# Basic line plot
ggplot(data=economics, aes(x = date, y = pop))+
  geom_line()

# Plot a subset of the data
ss <- subset(economics, date > as.Date("2006-1-1"))
ggplot(data = ss, aes(x = date, y = pop)) + geom_line()
```

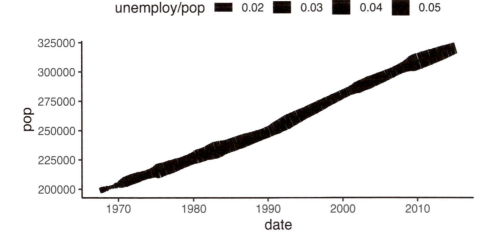

Change line size :

```r
ggplot(data = economics, aes(x = date, y = pop)) +
  geom_line(aes(size = unemploy/pop))
```

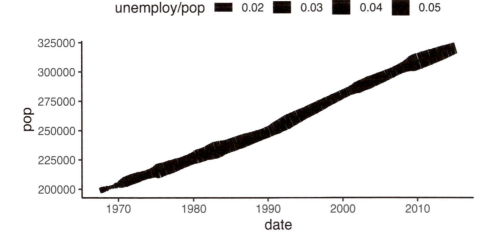

Plot multiple time series data:

```r
ggplot(economics, aes(x=date)) +
  geom_line(aes(y = psavert), color = "darkred") +
  geom_line(aes(y = uempmed), color="steelblue", linetype="twodash")
```

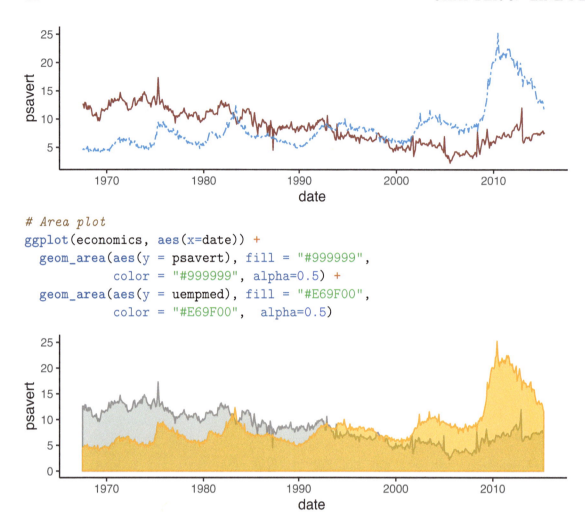

```
# Area plot
ggplot(economics, aes(x=date)) +
  geom_area(aes(y = psavert), fill = "#999999",
            color = "#999999", alpha=0.5) +
  geom_area(aes(y = uempmed), fill = "#E69F00",
            color = "#E69F00",  alpha=0.5)
```

## 8.9   Conclusion

This article shows how to create line plots using the ggplot2 package.

# Chapter 9

# Barplot

**Barplot** (also known as Bar Graph or Column Graph) is used to show discrete, numerical comparisons across categories. One axis of the chart shows the specific categories being compared and the other axis represents a discrete value scale.

This article describes how to create a **barplot** using the ggplot2 R package.

You will learn how to:

- Create basic and grouped barplots
- Add labels to a barplot
- Change the bar line and fill colors by group

## 9.1 Key R functions

- Key function: `geom_col()` for creating bar plots. The heights of the bars represent values in the data.
- Key arguments to customize the plot:
    - `color`, `fill`: bar border and fill color
    - `width`: bar width

## 9.2 Data preparation

We'll create two data frames derived from the `ToothGrowth` datasets.

```
df <- data.frame(dose=c("D0.5", "D1", "D2"),
            len=c(4.2, 10, 29.5))

head(df)

##   dose  len
## 1 D0.5  4.2
## 2   D1 10.0
## 3   D2 29.5
```

```r
df2 <- data.frame(supp=rep(c("VC", "OJ"), each=3),
                  dose=rep(c("D0.5", "D1", "D2"),2),
                  len=c(6.8, 15, 33, 4.2, 10, 29.5))

head(df2)

##    supp dose  len
## 1    VC D0.5  6.8
## 2    VC   D1 15.0
## 3    VC   D2 33.0
## 4    OJ D0.5  4.2
## 5    OJ   D1 10.0
## 6    OJ   D2 29.5
```

- len: Tooth length
- dose: Dose in milligrams (0.5, 1, 2)
- supp: Supplement type (VC or OJ)

## 9.3   Loading required R package

Load the ggplot2 package and set the default theme to `theme_classic()` with the legend at the top of the plot:

```r
library(ggplot2)
theme_set(
  theme_classic() +
    theme(legend.position = "top")
  )
```

## 9.4   Basic barplots

We start by creating a simple **barplot** (named **f**) using the *df* data set:

```r
f <- ggplot(df, aes(x = dose, y = len))

# Basic bar plot
f + geom_col()

# Change fill color and add labels at the top (vjust = -0.3)
f + geom_col(fill = "#0073C2FF") +
  geom_text(aes(label = len), vjust = -0.3)

# Label inside bars, vjust = 1.6
f + geom_col(fill = "#0073C2FF")+
  geom_text(aes(label = len), vjust = 1.6, color = "white")
```

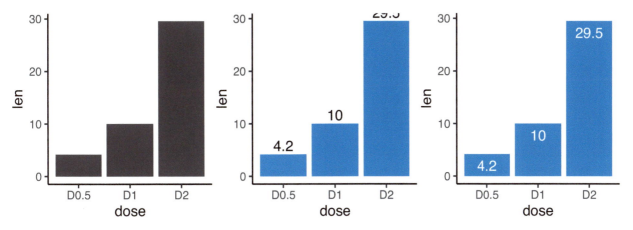

Note that, it's possible to change the width of bars using the argument `width` (e.g.: width = 0.5)

## 9.5   Change barplot colors by groups

We'll change the barplot line and fill color by the variable `dose` group levels. To set a palette of custom color the function `scale_color_manual()` is used.

```
# Change barplot line colors by groups
f + geom_col(aes(color = dose), fill = "white") +
  scale_color_manual(values = c("#00AFBB", "#E7B800", "#FC4E07"))
```

```
# Change barplot fill colors by groups
f + geom_col(aes(fill = dose)) +
  scale_fill_manual(values = c("#00AFBB", "#E7B800", "#FC4E07"))
```

## 9.6   Barplot with multiple groups

**Create stacked and dodged bar plots.** Use the functions `scale_color_manual()` and `scale_fill_manual()` to set manually the bars border line colors and area fill colors.

```r
# Stacked bar plots of y = counts by x = cut,
# colored by the variable color
ggplot(df2, aes(x = dose, y = len)) +
  geom_col(aes(color = supp, fill = supp), position = position_stack()) +
  scale_color_manual(values = c("#0073C2FF", "#EFC000FF"))+
  scale_fill_manual(values = c("#0073C2FF", "#EFC000FF"))

# Use position = position_dodge()
p <- ggplot(df2, aes(x = dose, y = len)) +
  geom_col(aes(color = supp, fill = supp), position = position_dodge(0.8), width = 0.7) +
  scale_color_manual(values = c("#0073C2FF", "#EFC000FF"))+
  scale_fill_manual(values = c("#0073C2FF", "#EFC000FF"))
p
```

Note that, `position_stack()` automatically stack values in the reverse order of the group aesthetic. This default ensures that bar colors align with the default legend. You can change this behavior by using `position = position_stack(reverse = TRUE)`.

**Add labels to a dodged barplot:**

```r
p + geom_text(
  aes(label = len, group = supp),
  position = position_dodge(0.8),
  vjust = -0.3, size = 3.5
)
```

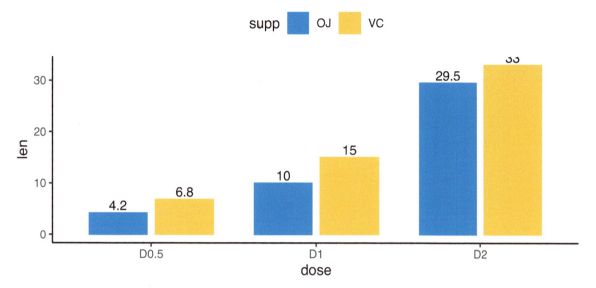

**Add labels to a stacked bar plots**. 4 steps required to compute the position of text labels:

- Group the data by the dose variable
- Sort the data by `dose` and `supp` columns. As `position_stack()` reverse the group order, `supp` column should be sorted in descending order.
- Calculate the cumulative sum of `len` for each `dose` category. Used as the y coordinates of labels. To put the label in the middle of the bars, we'll use `cumsum(len) - 0.5 * len`.
- Create the bar graph and add labels

```r
# Arrange/sort and compute cumulative summs
library(dplyr)
 df2 <- df2 %>%
  group_by(dose) %>%
  arrange(dose, desc(supp)) %>%
  mutate(lab_ypos = cumsum(len) - 0.5 * len)
df2
```

```
## # A tibble: 6 x 4
## # Groups:   dose [3]
##    supp  dose    len lab_ypos
##    <fct> <fct> <dbl>    <dbl>
## 1 VC    D0.5    6.8      3.4
## 2 OJ    D0.5    4.2      8.9
## 3 VC    D1     15        7.5
## 4 OJ    D1     10       20
## 5 VC    D2     33       16.5
## 6 OJ    D2     29.5     47.8
```

```r
# Create stacked bar graphs with labels
ggplot(data = df2, aes(x = dose, y = len)) +
  geom_col(aes(fill = supp), width = 0.7)+
  geom_text(aes(y = lab_ypos, label = len, group =supp), color = "white") +
  scale_color_manual(values = c("#0073C2FF", "#EFC000FF"))+
  scale_fill_manual(values = c("#0073C2FF", "#EFC000FF"))
```

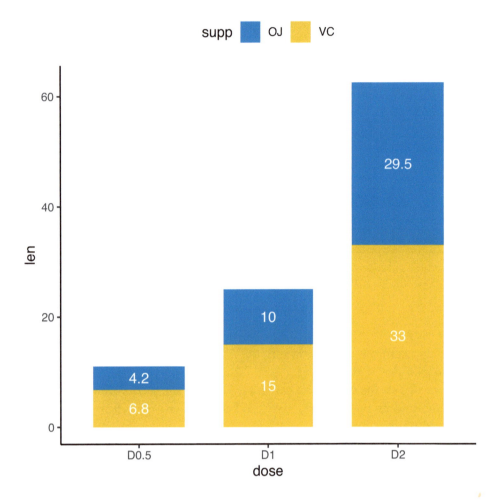

## 9.7   Conclusion

This article describes how to create and customize barplot using the ggplot2 R package.

# Chapter 10

# Error Bars

## 10.1 Introduction

**Error Bars** are used to visualize the variability of the plotted data. Error Bars can be applied to graphs such as, Dot Plots, Barplots or Line Graphs, to provide an additional layer of detail on the presented data.

Generally, Error bars are used to show either the standard deviation, standard error, confidence intervals or interquartile range.

The length of an Error Bar helps reveal the uncertainty of a data point: a short Error Bar shows that values are concentrated, signalling that the plotted average value is more likely, while a long Error Bar would indicate that the values are more spread out and less reliable.

This article describes how to add error bars into a plot using the **ggplot2** R package. You will learn how to create bar plots and line plots with error bars

## 10.2 Loading required R package

Load the ggplot2 package and set the default theme to `theme_classic()` with the legend at the top of the plot:

```
library(ggplot2)
theme_set(
  theme_classic() +
    theme(legend.position = "top")
  )
```

## 10.3 Data preparation

- Prepare the data: `ToothGrowth` data set.

```
df <- ToothGrowth
df$dose <- as.factor(df$dose)
head(df, 3)
```

```
##    len supp dose
## 1  4.2   VC  0.5
## 2 11.5   VC  0.5
## 3  7.3   VC  0.5
```

- Compute summary statistics for the variable `len` organized into groups by the variable `dose`:

```r
library(dplyr)
df.summary <- df %>%
  group_by(dose) %>%
  summarise(
    sd = sd(len, na.rm = TRUE),
    len = mean(len)
  )
df.summary
```

```
## # A tibble: 3 x 3
##   dose      sd   len
##   <fct> <dbl> <dbl>
## 1 0.5    4.50  10.6
## 2 1      4.42  19.7
## 3 2      3.77  26.1
```

## 10.4   Key R functions and error plot types

Key functions to create error plots using the summary statistics data:

- `geom_crossbar()` for hollow bar with middle indicated by horizontal line
- `geom_errorbar()` for error bars
- `geom_errorbarh()` for horizontal error bars
- `geom_linerange()` for drawing an interval represented by a vertical line
- `geom_pointrange()` for creating an interval represented by a vertical line, with a point in the middle.

Start by initializing ggplot with the summary statistics data:

- Specify x and y as usually
- Specify `ymin = len-sd` and `ymax = len+sd` to add lower and upper error bars. If you want only to add upper error bars but not the lower ones, use `ymin = len` (instead of `len-sd`) and `ymax = len+sd`.

```r
# Initialize ggplot with data
f <- ggplot(
  df.summary,
  aes(x = dose, y = len, ymin = len-sd, ymax = len+sd)
  )
```

Possible error plots:

**f + geom_crossbar()**  **f + geom_errorbar()**   **f + geom_linerange()**  **f + geom_pointrange()**

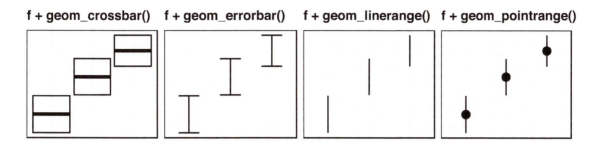

## 10.5   Basic error bars

Create simple error plots:

```
# Vertical line with point in the middle
f + geom_pointrange()
```

```
# Standard error bars
f + geom_errorbar(width = 0.2) +
  geom_point(size = 1.5)
```

Create horizontal error bars. Put `dose` on y axis and `len` on x-axis. Specify `xmin` and `xmax`.

```
# Horizontal error bars with mean points
# Change the color by groups
ggplot(df.summary, aes(x = len, y = dose, xmin = len-sd, xmax = len+sd)) +
  geom_point() +
  geom_errorbarh(height=.2)
```

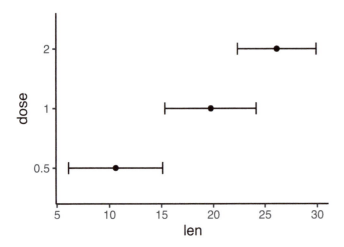

- Add jitter points (representing individual points), dot plots and violin plots. For this, you should initialize ggplot with original data (`df`) and specify the `df.summary` data in the error plot function, here `geom_pointrange()`.

```
# Combine with jitter points
ggplot(df, aes(dose, len)) +
  geom_jitter(position = position_jitter(0.2), color = "darkgray") +
  geom_pointrange(aes(ymin = len-sd, ymax = len+sd),data = df.summary)


# Combine with violin plots
ggplot(df, aes(dose, len)) +
  geom_violin(color = "darkgray", trim = FALSE) +
  geom_pointrange(aes(ymin = len-sd, ymax = len+sd), data = df.summary)
```

- Create basic bar/line plots of mean +/- error. So we need only the `df.summary` data. :
    1. Add lower and upper error bars for the line plot: `ymin = len-sd` and `ymax = len+sd`.
    2. Add only upper error bars for the bar plot: `ymin = len` (instead of `len-sd`) and `ymax = len+sd`.

Note that, for line plot, you should always specify `group = 1` in the `aes()`, when you have one group of line.

```r
# (1) Line plot
ggplot(df.summary, aes(dose, len)) +
  geom_line(aes(group = 1)) +
  geom_errorbar( aes(ymin = len-sd, ymax = len+sd),width = 0.2) +
  geom_point(size = 2)

# (2) Bar plot
ggplot(df.summary, aes(dose, len)) +
  geom_col(fill = "lightgray", color = "black") +
  geom_errorbar(aes(ymin = len, ymax = len+sd), width = 0.2)
```

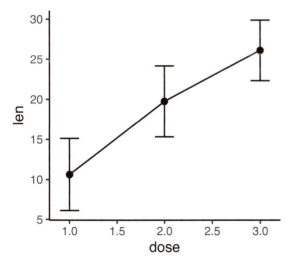

For line plot, you might want to treat x-axis as numeric:

```r
df.sum2 <- df.summary
df.sum2$dose <- as.numeric(df.sum2$dose)
ggplot(df.sum2, aes(dose, len)) +
  geom_line() +
  geom_errorbar( aes(ymin = len-sd, ymax = len+sd),width = 0.2) +
  geom_point(size = 2)
```

- Bar plots and line plots + jitter points. We need the original `df` data for the jitter points and the `df.summary` data for the other `geom` layers.
    1. For the line plot: First, add jitter points, then add lines + error bars + mean points on top of the jitter points.
    2. For the bar plot: First, add the bar plot, then add jitter points + error bars on top of the bars.

```r
# (1) Create a line plot of means +
# individual jitter points + error bars
ggplot(df, aes(dose, len)) +
  geom_jitter( position = position_jitter(0.2), color = "darkgray") +
  geom_line(aes(group = 1), data = df.summary) +
  geom_errorbar(
    aes(ymin = len-sd, ymax = len+sd),
    data = df.summary, width = 0.2) +
  geom_point(data = df.summary, size = 2)


# (2) Bar plots of means + individual jitter points + errors
ggplot(df, aes(dose, len)) +
  geom_col(data = df.summary, fill = NA, color = "black") +
  geom_jitter( position = position_jitter(0.2), color = "black") +
  geom_errorbar( aes(ymin = len-sd, ymax = len+sd),
                 data = df.summary, width = 0.2)
```

## 10.6  Grouped error bars

Case of one continuous variable (`len`) and two grouping variables (`dose`, `supp`).

- Compute the summary statistics of `len` grouped by `dose` and `supp`:

```r
library(dplyr)
df.summary2 <- df %>%
  group_by(dose, supp) %>%
  summarise(
```

```
    sd = sd(len),
    len = mean(len)
  )
df.summary2
```

```
## # A tibble: 6 x 4
## # Groups:   dose [3]
##    dose  supp    sd   len
##    <fct> <fct> <dbl> <dbl>
## 1 0.5   OJ     4.46 13.2
## 2 0.5   VC     2.75  7.98
## 3 1     OJ     3.91 22.7
## 4 1     VC     2.52 16.8
## 5 2     OJ     2.66 26.1
## 6 2     VC     4.80 26.1
```

- Create error plots for multiple groups:
  1. pointrange colored by groups (supp)
  2. standard error bars + mean points colored by groups (supp)

```
# (1) Pointrange: Vertical line with point in the middle
ggplot(df.summary2, aes(dose, len)) +
  geom_pointrange(
    aes(ymin = len-sd, ymax = len+sd, color = supp),
    position = position_dodge(0.3)
    )+
  scale_color_manual(values = c("#00AFBB", "#E7B800"))
```

```
# (2) Standard error bars
ggplot(df.summary2, aes(dose, len)) +
  geom_errorbar(
    aes(ymin = len-sd, ymax = len+sd, color = supp),
    position = position_dodge(0.3), width = 0.2
    )+
  geom_point(aes(color = supp), position = position_dodge(0.3)) +
  scale_color_manual(values = c("#00AFBB", "#E7B800"))
```

- Create simple line/bar plots for multiple groups.
  1. Line plots: change linetype by groups (**supp**)
  2. Bar plots: change fill color by groups (**supp**)

```
# (1) Line plot + error bars
ggplot(df.summary2, aes(dose, len)) +
  geom_line(aes(linetype = supp, group = supp))+
  geom_point()+
  geom_errorbar(
    aes(ymin = len-sd, ymax = len+sd, group = supp),
    width = 0.2
    )
```

```
# (2) Bar plots + upper error bars.
ggplot(df.summary2, aes(dose, len)) +
  geom_col(aes(fill = supp), position = position_dodge(0.8), width = 0.7)+
  geom_errorbar(
    aes(ymin = len, ymax = len+sd, group = supp),
    width = 0.2, position = position_dodge(0.8)
    )+
  scale_fill_manual(values = c("grey80", "grey30"))
```

- Add jitter points:

```
# Line plots with jittered points
ggplot(df, aes(dose, len, color = supp)) +
  geom_jitter(position = position_jitter(0.2)) +
  geom_line(aes(group = supp),data = df.summary2) +
  geom_errorbar(aes(ymin = len-sd, ymax = len+sd), data = df.summary2, width = 0.2)+
  scale_color_manual(values = c("#00AFBB", "#E7B800")) +
  theme(legend.position = "top")
```

```
# Bar plots + jittered points + error bars
ggplot(df, aes(dose, len, color = supp)) +
  geom_col(data = df.summary2, position = position_dodge(0.8),
           width = 0.7, fill = "white") +
  geom_jitter(
```

```
    position = position_jitterdodge(jitter.width = 0.2, dodge.width = 0.8)
    ) +
geom_errorbar(
    aes(ymin = len-sd, ymax = len+sd), data = df.summary2,
    width = 0.2, position = position_dodge(0.8)
    )+
scale_color_manual(values = c("#00AFBB", "#E7B800")) +
theme(legend.position = "top")
```

## 10.7  Conclusion

This article describes how to add error bars to plots created using the ggplot2 R package.

# Chapter 11

# Density Plot

A **density plot** is an alternative to Histogram used for visualizing the distribution of a continuous variable.

The peaks of a Density Plot help to identify where values are concentrated over the interval of the continuous variable.

Compared to Histograms, Density Plots are better at finding the distribution shape because they are re not affected by the number of bins used (each bar used in a typical histogram).

For example, a Histogram with only 4 bins wouldn't produce a distinguishable enough shape of distribution as a 30-bin Histogram would. However, with Density Plots, this isn't an issue.

This article describes how to create density plots using the **ggplot2** R package.

## 11.1 Key R functions

- Key function: `geom_density()` (for density plots).
- Key arguments to customize the plots:
  - `color, size, linetype`: change the line color, size and type, respectively
  - `fill`: change the areas fill color (for bar plots, histograms and density plots)
  - `alpha`: create a semi-transparent color.

## 11.2 Data preparation

Create some data (`wdata`) containing the weights by sex (M for male; F for female):

```
set.seed(1234)
wdata = data.frame(
      sex = factor(rep(c("F", "M"), each=200)),
      weight = c(rnorm(200, 55), rnorm(200, 58))
      )

head(wdata, 4)

##   sex weight
```

```
## 1   F    53.8
## 2   F    55.3
## 3   F    56.1
## 4   F    52.7
```

Compute the mean weight by sex using the **dplyr** package. First, the data is grouped by sex and then summarized by computing the mean weight by groups. The operator **%>%** is used to combine multiple operations:

```
library("dplyr")
mu <- wdata %>%
  group_by(sex) %>%
  summarise(grp.mean = mean(weight))
mu
```

```
## # A tibble: 2 x 2
##   sex   grp.mean
##   <fct>    <dbl>
## 1 F         54.9
## 2 M         58.1
```

## 11.3  Loading required R package

Load the ggplot2 package and set the default theme to **theme_classic()** with the legend at the top of the plot:

```
library(ggplot2)
theme_set(
  theme_classic() +
    theme(legend.position = "top")
  )
```

## 11.4  Basic density plots

We start by creating a plot, named **a**, that we'll finish in the next section by adding a layer using the function **geom_density()**.

```
a <- ggplot(wdata, aes(x = weight))
```

The following R code creates some basic density plots with a vertical line corresponding to the mean value of the weight variable (**geom_vline()**):

```
# Basic density plots
# y axis scale = stat(density) (default behaviour)
a + geom_density() +
  geom_vline(aes(xintercept = mean(weight)), linetype = "dashed")

# Change y axis to count instead of density
a + geom_density(aes(y = stat(count)), fill = "lightgray") +
  geom_vline(aes(xintercept = mean(weight)), linetype = "dashed")
```

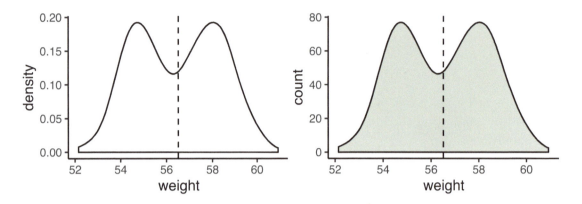

## 11.5   Change color by groups

The following R code will change the density plot line and fill color by groups. The functions `scale_color_manual()` and `scale_fill_manual()` are used to specify custom colors for each group.

We'll proceed as follow:

- Change areas fill and add line color by groups (sex)
- Add vertical mean lines using `geom_vline()`. Data: `mu`, which contains the mean values of weights by sex (computed in the previous section).
- Change color manually:
    - use `scale_color_manual()` or `scale_colour_manual()` for changing line color
    - use `scale_fill_manual()` for changing area fill colors.

```
# Change line color by sex
a + geom_density(aes(color = sex)) +
  scale_color_manual(values = c("#868686FF", "#EFC000FF"))


# Change fill color by sex and add mean line
# Use semi-transparent fill: alpha = 0.4
a + geom_density(aes(fill = sex), alpha = 0.4) +
  geom_vline(aes(xintercept = grp.mean, color = sex), data = mu, linetype = "dashed") +
  scale_color_manual(values = c("#868686FF", "#EFC000FF"))+
  scale_fill_manual(values = c("#868686FF", "#EFC000FF"))
```

# Chapter 12

# Histogram Plot

A **histogram plot** is an alternative to Density plot for visualizing the distribution of a continuous variable. This chart represents the distribution of a continuous variable by dividing into bins and counting the number of observations in each bin.

This article describes how to create Histogram plots using the **ggplot2** R package.

## 12.1  Key R functions

- Key function: `geom_histgram()` (for density plots).
- Key arguments to customize the plots:
  - `color, size, linetype`: change the line color, size and type, respectively
  - `fill`: change the areas fill color (for bar plots, histograms and density plots)
  - `alpha`: create a semi-transparent color.

## 12.2  Data preparation

Create some data (`wdata`) containing the weights by sex (M for male; F for female):

```
set.seed(1234)
wdata = data.frame(
        sex = factor(rep(c("F", "M"), each=200)),
        weight = c(rnorm(200, 55), rnorm(200, 58))
        )
```

```
head(wdata, 4)
```

```
##   sex weight
## 1   F   53.8
## 2   F   55.3
## 3   F   56.1
## 4   F   52.7
```

Compute the mean weight by sex using the `dplyr` package. First, the data is grouped by sex and then summarized by computing the mean weight by groups. The operator `%>%` is used to combine multiple operations:

```
library("dplyr")
mu <- wdata %>%
  group_by(sex) %>%
  summarise(grp.mean = mean(weight))
mu
```

```
## # A tibble: 2 x 2
##    sex   grp.mean
##    <fct>    <dbl>
## 1 F         54.9
## 2 M         58.1
```

## 12.3   Loading required R package

Load the ggplot2 package and set the default theme to `theme_classic()` with the legend at the top of the plot:

```
library(ggplot2)
theme_set(
  theme_classic() +
    theme(legend.position = "top")
  )
```

## 12.4   Basic histogram plots

We start by creating a plot, named **a**, that we'll finish in the next section by adding a layer using the function `geom_histogram()`.

```
a <- ggplot(wdata, aes(x = weight))
```

The following R code creates some basic density plots with a vertical line corresponding to the mean value of the weight variable (`geom_vline()`):

```
# Basic density plots
a + geom_histogram(bins = 30, color = "black", fill = "gray") +
  geom_vline(aes(xintercept = mean(weight)),
             linetype = "dashed", size = 0.6)
```

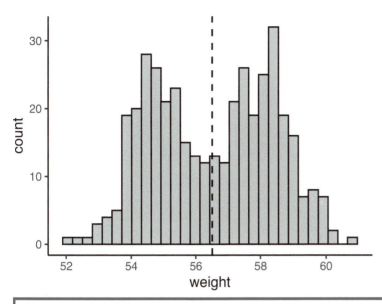

> Note that, by default:
>
> - By default, `geom_histogram()` uses 30 bins - this might not be good default. You can change the number of bins (e.g.: bins = 50) or the bin width (e.g.: binwidth = 0.5)
> - The y axis corresponds to the count of weight values. If you want to change the plot in order to have the density on y axis, specify the argument `y = ..density..` in `aes()`.

## 12.5 Change color by groups

The following R code will change the histogram plot line and fill color by groups. The functions `scale_color_manual()` and `scale_fill_manual()` are used to specify custom colors for each group.

We'll proceed as follow:

- Change areas fill and add line color by groups (sex)
- Add vertical mean lines using `geom_vline()`. Data: `mu`, which contains the mean values of weights by sex (computed in the previous section).
- Change color manually:
    - use `scale_color_manual()` or `scale_colour_manual()` for changing line color
    - use `scale_fill_manual()` for changing area fill colors.
- Adjust the position of histogram bars by using the argument `position`. Allowed values: "identity", "stack", "dodge". Default value is "stack".

```
# Change line color by sex
a + geom_histogram(aes(color = sex), fill = "white",
                position = "identity") +
  scale_color_manual(values = c("#00AFBB", "#E7B800"))


# change fill and outline color manually
a + geom_histogram(aes(color = sex, fill = sex),
                alpha = 0.4, position = "identity") +
```

```
scale_fill_manual(values = c("#00AFBB", "#E7B800")) +
scale_color_manual(values = c("#00AFBB", "#E7B800"))
```

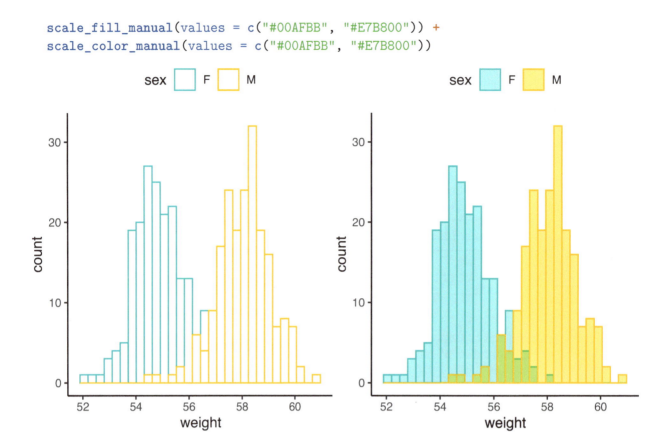

## 12.6   Combine histogram and density plots

- Plot histogram with density values on y-axis (instead of count values).
- Add density plot with transparent density plot

```
# Histogram with density plot
a + geom_histogram(aes(y = stat(density)),
                 colour="black", fill="white") +
  geom_density(alpha = 0.2, fill = "#FF6666")



# Color by groups
a + geom_histogram(aes(y = stat(density), color = sex),
                 fill = "white",position = "identity")+
  geom_density(aes(color = sex), size = 1) +
  scale_color_manual(values = c("#868686FF", "#EFC000FF"))
```

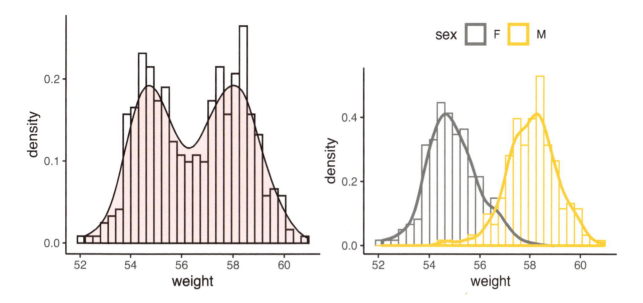

## 12.7   Conclusion

This article describes how to create histogram plots using the ggplot2 package.

# Chapter 13

# QQPlot

A **Quantile-quantile plot** (or **QQPlot**) is used to check whether a given data follows normal distribution.

The data is assumed to be normally distributed when the points approximately follow the 45-degree reference line.

This article describes how to create a qqplot in R using the **ggplot2** package.

## 13.1  Key R functions

- Key function: `stat_qq()`.
- Key arguments: `color`, `shape` and `size` to change point color, shape and size.

## 13.2  Data preparation

Create some data (`wdata`) containing the weights by sex (M for male; F for female):

```r
set.seed(1234)
wdata = data.frame(
        sex = factor(rep(c("F", "M"), each=200)),
        weight = c(rnorm(200, 55), rnorm(200, 58))
        )

# head(wdata, 4)
```

## 13.3  Loading required R package

Load the ggplot2 package and set the default theme to `theme_minimal()` with the legend at the top of the plot:

```r
library(ggplot2)
theme_set(
  theme_minimal() +
```

```
    theme(legend.position = "top")
  )
```

## 13.4  Create qqplots

Create a qq-plot of weight. Change color by groups (sex)

```
ggplot(wdata, aes(sample = weight)) +
  stat_qq(aes(color = sex)) +
  scale_color_manual(values = c("#00AFBB", "#E7B800"))+
  labs(y = "Weight")
```

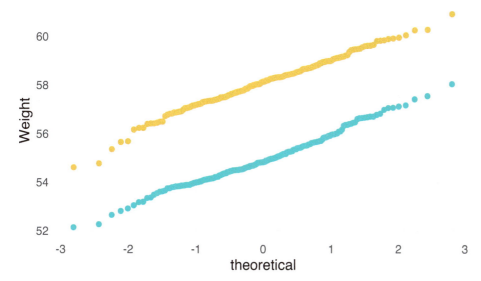

Alternative plot using the function `ggqqplot()` [in ggpubr]. The 95% confidence band is shown by default.

```
library(ggpubr)
ggqqplot(wdata, x = "weight",
    color = "sex",
    palette = c("#0073C2FF", "#FC4E07"),
    ggtheme = theme_pubclean())
```

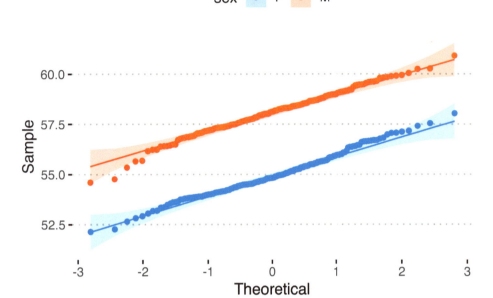

## 13.5   Conclusion

This article shows how to create a qqplot using the ggplot2 and the ggpubr package.

# Chapter 14

# ECDF Plot

**ECDF** (or **Empirical cumulative distribution function**) provides an alternative visualization of distribution. It reports for any given number the percent of individuals that are below that threshold.

This article describes how to create an ECDF in R using the function `stat_ecdf()` in **ggplot2** package.

## 14.1 Data preparation

Create some data (`wdata`) containing the weights by sex (M for male; F for female):

```r
set.seed(1234)
wdata = data.frame(
        sex = factor(rep(c("F", "M"), each=200)),
        weight = c(rnorm(200, 55), rnorm(200, 58))
        )

# head(wdata, 4)
```

## 14.2 Loading required R package

Load the ggplot2 package and set the default theme to `theme_minimal()` with the legend at the top of the plot:

```r
library(ggplot2)
theme_set(
  theme_minimal() +
    theme(legend.position = "top")
  )
```

## 14.3   Create ECDF plots

```
# Another option for geom = "point"
ggplot(wdata, aes(x = weight)) +
  stat_ecdf(aes(color = sex,linetype = sex),
            geom = "step", size = 1.5) +
  scale_color_manual(values = c("#00AFBB", "#E7B800"))+
  labs(y = "f(weight)")
```

In the above plots, you can see that:

- about 25% of our females are shorter than 50 inches
- about 50% of males are shorter than 58 inches

## 14.4   Conclusion

This article shows how to create an ECDF plot using the ggplot2 R package.

# Chapter 15

# Multiple GGPlots into a Figure

## 15.1  Introduction

This article describes how to combine **multiple ggplots** into a figure. To achieve this task, there are many R function/packages, including:

- grid.arrange() [gridExtra package]
- plot_grid() [cowplot package]
- plot_layout() [patchwork package]
- ggarrange() [ggpubr package]

The function `ggarrange()` [ggpubr] is one of the easiest solution for arranging multiple ggplots.

Here, you will learn how to use:

- ggplot2 facet functions for creating multiple panel figures that share the same axes
- ggarrange() function for combining independent ggplots

## 15.2  Loading required R packages

Load the ggplot2 package and set the default theme to `theme_bw()` with the legend at the top of the plot:

```
library(ggplot2)
library("ggpubr")
theme_set(
  theme_bw() +
    theme(legend.position = "top")
  )
```

## 15.3  Basic ggplot

Create a box plot filled by groups:

```r
# Load data and convert dose to a factor variable
data("ToothGrowth")
ToothGrowth$dose <- as.factor(ToothGrowth$dose)
# Box plot
p <- ggplot(ToothGrowth, aes(x = dose, y = len)) +
  geom_boxplot(aes(fill = supp), position = position_dodge(0.9)) +
  scale_fill_manual(values = c("#00AFBB", "#E7B800"))
p
```

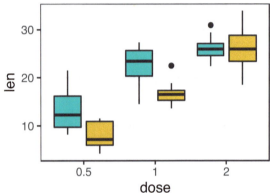

## 15.4   Multiple panels figure using ggplot facet

Facets divide a ggplot into subplots based on the values of one or more categorical variables.

When you are creating multiple plots that share axes, you should consider using facet functions from ggplot2

You write your ggplot2 code as if you were putting all of the data onto one plot, and then you use one of the faceting functions to indicate how to slice up the graph.

There are two main facet functions in the ggplot2 package:

1. `facet_grid()`, which layouts panels in a grid. It creates a matrix of panels defined by row and column faceting variables
2. `facet_wrap()`, which wraps a 1d sequence of panels into 2d. This is generally a better use of screen space than facet_grid() because most displays are roughly rectangular.

### 15.4.1   Using facet_grid

1. **Facet with one discrete variable.** Split by the levels of the group "supp"

```r
# Split in vertical direction
p + facet_grid(rows = vars(supp))
```

```r
# Split in horizontal direction
p + facet_grid(cols = vars(supp))
```

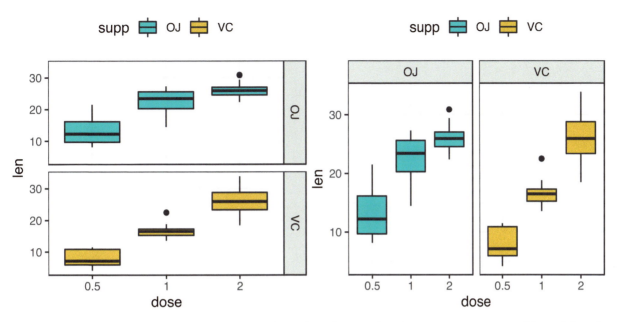

2. **Facet with multiple variables.** Split by the levels of two grouping variables: "dose" and "supp"

```
# Facet by two variables: dose and supp.
# Rows are dose and columns are supp
p + facet_grid(rows = vars(dose), cols = vars(supp))
```

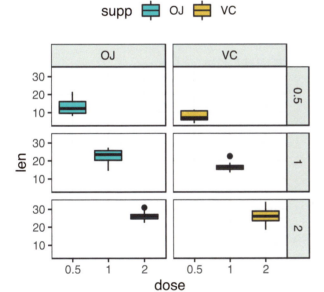

## 15.4.2 Using facet_wrap

**facet_wrap**: Facets can be placed side by side using the function `facet_wrap()` as follow :

```
p + facet_wrap(vars(dose))
```

```
p + facet_wrap(vars(dose), ncol=2)
```

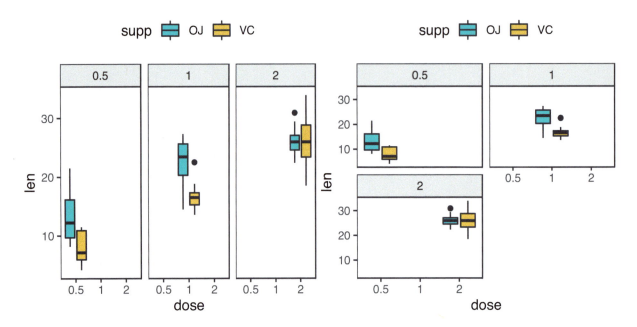

### 15.4.3  Facet scales

By default, all the panels have the same scales (`scales="fixed"`). They can be made independent, by setting scales to `free`, `free_x`, or `free_y`.

```r
p + facet_grid(rows = vars(dose), cols = vars(supp), scales = "free")
```

## 15.5  Combine multiple ggplots using ggarrange()

### 15.5.1  Create some basic plots

```r
# 0. Define custom color palette and prepare the data
my3cols <- c("#E7B800", "#2E9FDF", "#FC4E07")
ToothGrowth$dose <- as.factor(ToothGrowth$dose)

# 1. Create a box plot (bp)
p <- ggplot(ToothGrowth, aes(x = dose, y = len))
bxp <- p + geom_boxplot(aes(color = dose)) +
  scale_color_manual(values = my3cols)

# 2. Create a dot plot (dp)
dp <- p + geom_dotplot(aes(color = dose, fill = dose),
                      binaxis='y', stackdir='center') +
  scale_color_manual(values = my3cols) +
  scale_fill_manual(values = my3cols)

# 3. Create a line plot
lp <- ggplot(economics, aes(x = date, y = psavert)) +
  geom_line(color = "#E46726")
```

## 15.5.2   Combine the plots on one page

```
figure <- ggarrange(bxp, dp, lp,
                    labels = c("A", "B", "C"),
                    ncol = 2, nrow = 2)
figure
```

## 15.5.3   Change column and row span of a plot

We'll use nested **ggarrange()** functions to change column/row span of plots.  For example, using the R code below:

- the line plot (lp) will live in the first row and spans over two columns
- the box plot (bxp) and the dot plot (dp) will be first arranged and will live in the second row with two different columns

```
ggarrange(
  lp,                    # First row with line plot
  # Second row with box and dot plots
  ggarrange(bxp, dp, ncol = 2, labels = c("B", "C")),
  nrow = 2,
  labels = "A"           # Label of the line plot
  )
```

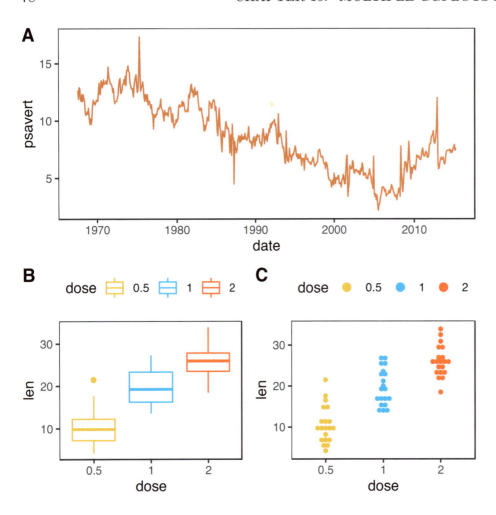

## 15.5.4  Use shared legend for combined ggplots

To place a common unique legend in the margin of the arranged plots, the function `ggarrange()` [in ggpubr] can be used with the following arguments:

- `common.legend = TRUE`: place a common legend in a margin
- `legend`: specify the legend position. Allowed values include one of c("top", "bottom", "left", "right")

```
ggarrange(
  bxp, dp, labels = c("A", "B"),
  common.legend = TRUE, legend = "bottom"
)
```

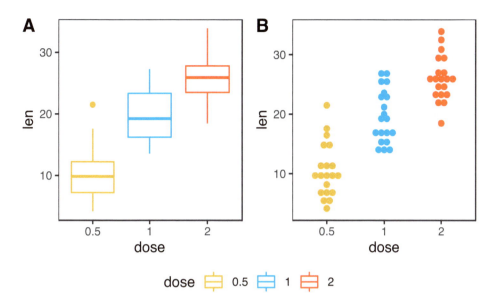

### 15.5.5 Combine the plots over multiple pages

If you have a long list of ggplots, say n = 20 plots, you may want to arrange the plots and to place them on multiple pages. With 4 plots per page, you need 5 pages to hold the 20 plots.

The function `ggarrange()` [ggpubr] provides a convenient solution to arrange multiple ggplots over multiple pages. After specifying the arguments `nrow` and `ncol`, `ggarrange()`' computes automatically the number of pages required to hold the list of the plots. It returns a list of arranged ggplots.

For example the following R code,

```
multi.page <- ggarrange(bxp, dp, lp, bxp,
                        nrow = 1, ncol = 2)
```

returns a list of two pages with two plots per page. You can visualize each page as follow:

```
multi.page[[1]] # Visualize page 1
multi.page[[2]] # Visualize page 2
```

You can also export the arranged plots to a pdf file using the function `ggexport()` [ggpubr]:

```
ggexport(multi.page, filename = "multi.page.ggplot2.pdf")
```

See the PDF file: Multi.page.ggplot2[1]

### 15.5.6 Export the arranged plots

R function: `ggexport()` [in ggpubr].

- Export the arranged figure to a pdf, eps or png file (one figure per page).

```
ggexport(figure, filename = "figure1.pdf")
```

- It's also possible to arrange the plots (2 plot per page) when exporting them.

---

[1]http://www.slideshare.net/kassambara/multipageggplot2

Export individual plots to a pdf file (one plot per page):

```
ggexport(bxp, dp, lp, bxp, filename = "test.pdf")
```

Arrange and export. Specify the nrow and ncol arguments to display multiple plots on the same page:

```
ggexport(bxp, dp, lp, bxp, filename = "test.pdf",
         nrow = 2, ncol = 1)
```

## 15.6   Conclusion

This article describes how to create a multiple plots figure using the ggplot2 facet functions and the ggarrange() function available in the ggpubr package. We also show how to export the arranged plots.

# Bibliography

Wickham, H., Chang, W., Henry, L., Pedersen, T. L., Takahashi, K., Wilke, C., Woo, K., and Yutani, H. (2019). *ggplot2: Create Elegant Data Visualisations Using the Grammar of Graphics*. R package version 3.2.0.

# Index

Bar plots, 54
Bubble Chart, 20

Facet, 74

Line plots, 54

Numeric x-axis in line plots, 55

Stripcharts, 35

www.ingramcontent.com/pod-product-compliance
Lightning Source LLC
Chambersburg PA
CBHW041434050326

40690CB00003B/542